MATHS PLUS
FROM HEINEMANN

Supporting Number

Activities for Teaching Assistants

Steve Mills and Hilary Koll

Heinemann

Halley Court, Jordan Hill, Oxford, OX2 8EJ
a division of Reed Educational and Professional Publishing Ltd
www.heinemann.co.uk

Heinemann is a registered trademark of Reed Educational and Professional Publishing Ltd

The text on pages 6–8 is taken from the NNS *Sample medium-term plans for mathematics*, published by the DfEE. Crown copyright is reproduced with the permission of the Controller of Her Majesty's Stationery Office.

ISBN 0435 03270 4

04   03   02   01   00
10 9 8 7 6 5 4 3 2 1

Typeset by Artistix, Thame, Oxon
Illustrated by Nick Schon
Printed and bound in Great Britain by Page Bros.

Contents

Introduction

For the teacher

Supporting Number has been written to support teaching assistants working with lower-ability children from Reception to Year 6. Each book contains 55 2-page teaching units which address the earlier objectives from the relevant NNS yearly teaching programme. The combination of practical activities and guidance helps to ensure that children get maximum benefit from the presence of an additional adult, while the easy-to-use photocopiable format includes space for the teaching assistant to provide you with focused feedback on children's strengths and weaknesses.

Discuss these lessons with the teaching assistant and involve them in planning where possible. It is intended that the activities follow your oral/mental starter and the whole-class teaching input. Encourage children from the teaching assistant's group to report back to the class during the plenary. The activities within a unit can be extended across more than one day and can be repeated throughout the year to further consolidate the mathematical ideas and help to prevent children from falling behind.

The teaching units follow the order suggested by the NNS *Sample medium-term plans for mathematics* (see pages 6–8). However, given that this is only a sample plan, the broader match to the *Framework* on page 9 lists all the units that relate to each content area, giving you the flexibility to deal with topics in a different order, and enabling you to find related activities.

For the teaching assistant

The teaching units contained in this book give information on:
- resources needed in the lesson
- words to use – appropriate vocabulary for children of this age and ability range
- things to note – points to watch for and to be aware of relating to language, mathematical skills and knowledge, and potential difficulties
- what to do – the activities, with questions to ask
- feedback – specific questions with space for you to write notes on the children's achievements, difficulties, and any other points of interest. This information can be of great value in providing the teacher with a detailed record of the children's work with you and helping them to plan more effectively for future lessons.

Maths doesn't have to be hard!

Many children find maths difficult and, as a result, can become anxious and negative towards it. Maths builds up in a way that means certain things need to be understood before sense can be made of what comes next, particularly in the case of number work. Numbers to 5 are learnt before numbers to 50, for example, and addition comes before multiplication. If children are moved on too quickly, they often fail to really understand and so fall behind. Many children need help and support to overcome their difficulties if they are to become confident with maths both in and out of school.

It's good to talk

Talking about maths is an excellent way of coming to understand it. Choosing words carefully and explaining things logically can help us to understand more clearly.
It can also help others who are listening and responding to clarify their understanding.

Children can be encouraged to talk about the maths they are doing in several ways:

Asking children to explain
▸ asking a child to explain how they worked something out
▸ asking children to suggest alternative strategies
▸ asking children to explain what they have done so far
▸ asking children to explain what they have done to a friend

As children discuss their work they will make mistakes. Try to avoid saying *No, that's wrong*, as doing so can make children reluctant to offer ideas next time. Instead, ask *How did you get that? Why do you think that?* or *Do we all agree?*
Listen carefully to children's explanations. They can tell you a lot about whether a child really understands. Encourage the other children to listen carefully, too.

Questioning
There are two types of question you can ask children. The first type, closed questions, have only one answer, for example *Three plus two equals …?* or *What are five sixes?* The second kind are called open questions and have more than one answer, for example *Tell me two numbers that add up to five.*
Here are some examples of both, showing how a closed question can be 'opened out':

Closed questions		Open questions
$6 + 4 = ?$	$\longrightarrow$	*What pairs of numbers add to make 10?*
$5 - 2 = ?$	$\longrightarrow$	*Give me two numbers with a difference of 3.*
Is 6 an even number?	$\longrightarrow$	*Tell me some even numbers you know.*

Asking an open question can tell you more about what a child understands than a closed one. For example, *What is 17 minus 5?* allows Jo to show you that she can do $17 - 5$. But that's all. She may be capable of $100 - 88$, but has no opportunity to show you. Closed questions put a ceiling on what a child can show. Open questions remove the ceiling, allowing children to really demonstrate what they can do:
If the answer is 12, what could the question be?

Questions can be asked at various times during an activity:

<table>
<tr><td>

At the beginning
What do you have to do?
What are you going to use?
What do you think the answer might roughly be?

</td><td>

During
Why did you choose to do it this way?
What will you do next?
Is there a quicker way?
Can you see a pattern?

</td></tr>
<tr><td>

If children get stuck
What have you done so far?
Would some cubes/pictures etc. help?
What did we do yesterday?
Can anyone else help him?

</td><td>

After
How did you work it out?
How did you check your answer?
What new words have you learnt?
What must you remember for tomorrow?

</td></tr>
</table>

Match to NNS Sample medium-term plan for Year 4

AUTUMN TERM

Oral and mental skills	Teaching unit
Recall addition and subtraction facts for each number up to 20.	4
Add/subtract a pair of two-digit numbers (not crossing 10 or 100 boundary).	8
Derive doubles of whole numbers to 50, corresponding halves.	6

NNS unit	Days	Topic	Objectives; children will be taught to:	Teaching unit
1	3	Place value, ordering, rounding	Read and write whole numbers to 10 000 in figures and words.	1
			Know what each digit represents and partition into Th H T U.	2
			Read and write the vocabulary of estimation.	3
			Estimate up to 250 objects.	
			Estimate a proportion (fraction).	
		Reading numbers from scales	Read scales to a suitable degree of accuracy.	
2–3	10	Understanding + and −	Consolidate understanding of relationship between addition/subtraction.	4
			Understand commutative law of addition.	
		Mental calculation strategies (+ and −)	Count on or back in repeated steps of 1, 10, 100.	5
			Identify near doubles.	6
			Count up through next multiple of 10, 100, 1000.	7
		Pencil and paper procedures (+ and −)	Use informal pencil and paper methods to support, record or explain addition and subtraction.	8
		Money and 'real-life' problems	Convert £ to p.	9
		Making decisions, checking results	Choose appropriate number operations and calculation methods to solve money or 'real-life' word problems with one/two steps.	
			Explain and record methods.	4
			Check with addition in a different order.	
4–6	13	Measures, including problems	Use, read, write *km, m, cm, mm* and *mile*.	
			Know and use relationships between units.	
			Know $\frac{1}{2}, \frac{1}{4}, \frac{3}{4}, \frac{1}{10}$ of 1 kilometre in *m*, 1 metre in *cm* or *mm*.	
			Suggest suitable units and equipment to estimate or measure length.	
			Record metres and centimetres using decimals, and other measurements using mixed units.	
			Convert up to 1000 cm to metres and vice versa.	
			Measure/calculate perimeter of rectangles and simple shapes *(cm)*.	
			Choose appropriate number operations and calculation methods to solve measurement word problems with one or more steps.	
			Explain and record methods.	
		Shape and space	Describe and visualize 3D and 2D shapes, inc. tetrahedron, heptagon.	
			Recognize equilateral and isosceles triangles.	
			Classify shapes (right angles, regularity, symmetry).	
			Recognize position on square grids with numbered lines.	
		Reasoning about shapes	Investigate general statements about shapes.	
7	2	Assess and review		

	Teaching unit
Recall multiplication facts in 2, 3, 4, 5 and 10 times tables, and derive division facts.	12
Multiply and divide whole numbers by 10 (and 100).	13

NNS unit	Days	Topic	Objectives; children will be taught to:	Teaching unit
8	5	Numbers and number sequences	Recognize, extend number sequences formed by counting from any number in steps of constant size, e.g. 25 to 500.	10
			Recognize odd and even numbers up to 1000 and some of their properties, e.g. sums, differences of pairs of odd/even numbers.	11
		Reasoning about numbers	Solve number puzzles, recognize patterns, generalize and predict.	
9–10	10	Understanding × and ÷	Extend understanding of × and ÷ and their relationship to each other and to + and −.	14
		Mental calculation strategies (× and ÷)	Use doubling and halving of two-digit numbers, e.g. ×4 = double, double; ×5 = ×10, halve; ×20 = ×10, double; ×8 = ×4, double; $\frac{1}{4}$ = half of one-half.	15
		Pencil and paper procedures (× and ÷)	Approximating first, use informal pencil and paper methods to multiply and divide.	16
		Money and 'real-life' problems	Choose appropriate number operations and calculation methods to solve money and 'real-life' word problems with one or more steps.	17
		Making decisions, checking results	Explain and record methods. Check with equivalent calculation.	
11	5	Fractions and decimals	Use fraction notation. Recognize fractions that are several parts of a whole, and mixed numbers.	18, 19
			Find fractions of shapes.	18
			Relate fractions to division and find simple fractions of quantities.	20
12	5	Understanding + and −	Consolidate understanding of subtraction as the inverse of addition.	21
		Mental calculation strategies (+ and −)	Find a small difference by counting up.	
			Use relationship between + and −.	
		Pencil and paper procedures (+ and −)	Develop written methods for + and − of whole numbers less than 1000.	22
		Time, including problems	Use, read, write vocabulary of time.	
			Read time to 1 min. on analogue/12-hour digital clock.	
			Use 9:53, a.m. and p.m.	
			Solve time word problems.	
13	5	Handling data	Solve a given problem by collecting, classifying, representing and interpreting data in tally charts, frequency tables, pictograms (symbols representing 2, 5, 10 units). Include use of computer.	
14	2	Assess and review		

SPRING TERM

Oral and mental skills	Teaching unit
Derive doubles of multiples of 10 to 500, corresponding halves.	23

NNS unit	Days	Topic	Objectives; children will be taught to:	Teaching unit
1	3	Place value, ordering, rounding	Multiply and divide an integer up to 1000 by 10; understand the effect.	24
			Read and write the vocabulary of comparing and ordering numbers.	25
			Use symbols = < > correctly.	
			Give a number lying between two others.	
			Use vocabulary of approximation.	
			Round any positive number less than 1000 to nearest 10.	26
		Reading numbers from scales	Recognize negative numbers in context: number line, thermometer.	27
2–4	15	Understanding + and –	Understand the principle (not the name) of the commutative law for +, not –.	28
		Mental calculation strategies (+ and –)	Add several small numbers by finding pairs that total 10, or 9 or 11.	
			Partition into tens and units, adding tens first.	29
			Add three two-digit multiples of 10.	
		Pencil and paper procedures (+ and –)	Develop/refine written methods for addition/subtraction, including money.	30
		Money and 'real-life' problems	Choose appropriate number operations and calculation methods to solve money and 'real-life' word problems with one or more steps.	31
		Making decisions, checking results	Explain working. Check with an equivalent calculation.	
5–6	8	Measures, and time, including problems	Estimate and check times using seconds, minutes, hours.	
			Measure and compare using kilograms and grams, and know and use the relationship between them.	
			Know $\frac{1}{4}$, $\frac{1}{2}$, $\frac{3}{4}$, and $\frac{1}{10}$ of 1 kg in grams.	
			Suggest suitable units and equipment to estimate or measure mass.	
			Read scales.	
			Record measurements to suitable degree of accuracy, using mixed units, or the nearest whole/half/quarter unit (e.g. 3·25 kg).	
			Measure and calculate area of rectangles and simple shapes, using counting methods and standard units (square centimetres).	
			Choose appropriate number operations and calculation methods to solve measurement word problems with one or more steps. Explain working.	
		Shape and space	Make shapes and discuss properties.	
			Visualize solid shapes from 2D drawings. Identify simple nets.	
			Recognise clockwise, anti-clockwise.	
			Start to draw, measure and order angles.	
			Use eight compass points.	
			Recognize horizontal and vertical lines.	
		Reasoning about shapes	Solve shape problems or puzzles. Explain reasoning and methods.	
7	2	Assess and review		

	Teaching unit
Add/subtract a pair of two-digit numbers (crossing 10 but not 100 boundary).	33
Derive addition pairs that total 100, multiples of 50 that total 1000.	34

NNS unit	Days	Topic	Objectives; children will be taught to:	Teaching unit
8	5	Numbers and number sequences	Recognize, extend number sequences formed by counting from any number in steps of constant size, extend beyond zero if counting back.	32
		Reasoning about numbers	Investigate general statements about familiar numbers.	35
			Explain methods and reasoning.	
9–10	10	Understanding × and ÷	Understand commutative and associative laws of multiplication.	
			Divide a whole number of £ by 2, 4, 5 or 10 to give £·p.	36
		Mental calculation strategies (× and ÷)	Use closely related facts, e.g. derive ×9 or ×11 from ×10, or derive ×6 from ×4 plus ×2.	37
		Pencil and paper procedures (× and ÷)	Partition and multiply.	38
			Develop and refine written methods for TU × U.	
		Money and 'real-life' problems Making decisions	Choose appropriate number operations and calculation methods to solve money and 'real-life' word problems with one or more steps. Explain working.	39
		Checking results	Check with inverse operation.	
11	5	Fractions and decimals	Recognize equivalence of simple fractions.	40
			Identify two fractions with total of 1.	41
			Compare a fraction with one half, and say whether it is greater or less.	40
			Use decimal notation for tenths, hundredths (money, metres and centimetres) and use in context. Round to the nearest £ or metre.	42, 43
			Convert £ to p, or metres to centimetres, and vice versa.	43
			Order decimals with two places.	44
12	5	Handling data	Solve a given problem by collecting, classifying, representing and interpreting data in bar charts; intervals labelled in twos, fives, tens, twenties. Include use of computer.	
13	2	Assess and review		

SUMMER TERM

NNS unit	Days	Topic	Objectives; children will be taught to:	Teaching unit
1	3	Place value, ordering, rounding	Begin to multiply whole numbers by 100.	45
			Order a set of whole numbers up to 10000.	46
			Round any positive integer to the nearest 10 or 100.	47
		Reading numbers from scales	Read a variety of scales and dials to a suitable degree of accuracy.	
2–3	10	Understanding + and –	Understand the principles of associative law of addition (not name).	
		Mental calculation strategies (+ and –)	Add or subtract the nearest multiple of 10 and adjust.	48
			Use number facts and place value to add/subtract mentally any pair of two-digit whole numbers.	
		Pencil and paper procedures (+ and –)	Develop and refine written methods for column addition/subtraction.	49
			Add more than two whole numbers less than 1000, and money.	
		Money and 'real-life' problems Making decisions, checking results	Choose appropriate operations and calculation methods to solve money and 'real-life' word problems with one or two steps. Explain working.	
			Check using knowledge of sums of odd/even numbers.	
4–6	13	Measures, including problems	Use, read, write *litre (l), millilitre (ml), pint*.	
			Know $\frac{1}{4}, \frac{1}{2}, \frac{3}{4}, \frac{1}{10}$ of 1 litre in ml.	
			Suggest suitable units and equipment to estimate or measure capacity.	
			Read scales.	
			Record measurements to suitable degree of accuracy, using mixed units, or the nearest whole/half/quarter unit (e.g. 3·25 litres).	
			Choose appropriate number operations and calculation methods to solve measurement word problems with one or more steps.	
			Explain working.	
		Shape and space	Sketch reflection of simple shape in a mirror.	
			Read and begin to write the vocabulary of movement.	
			Make and describe patterns involving translations.	
			Begin to measure angles in degrees.	
			Know whole turn, 360°, 4 right angles; quarter turn, 90°, 1 right angle; half turn, 180°, 2 right angles.	
			Recognize 45° as half a right angle.	
7	2	Assess and review		
8	5	Numbers and number sequences	Recognize multiples of 2, 3, 4, 5, 10, up to tenth multiple.	50
		Reasoning about numbers	Solve number problems and puzzles.	
			Explain methods and reasoning orally and in writing.	
9–10	10	Understanding × and ÷	Understand distributive law.	
			Round up or down after division.	51
		Mental calculation strategies (× and ÷)	Use relation between × and ÷.	52
			Use known facts to multiply and divide.	
		Pencil and paper procedures (× and ÷)	Develop and refine written methods for TU ÷ U.	53
		Money and 'real-life' problems Making decisions, checking results	Choose appropriate operations and calculation methods to solve money and 'real-life' word problems with one or more steps. Explain working. Check results by approximating.	
11	5	Fractions and decimals	Begin to use ideas of simple proportion.	
			Recognize the equivalence of decimal and fraction forms of one-half, one-quarter and tenths.	54
12	5	Understanding + and –	Consolidate understanding of addition and subtraction.	
		Mental calculation strategies (+ and –)	Add/subtract mentally any pair of two-digit whole numbers.	55
		Pencil and paper procedures (+ and –)	Refine column addition and subtraction.	
		Time, including problems	Read timetables and use this year's calendar.	
			Solve problems involving time.	
13	5	Handling data	Solve a given problem by collecting, classifying, representing and interpreting data in Venn and Carroll diagrams: two criteria. Use a computer and a branching tree program to sort shapes or numbers.	
14	2	Assess and review		

NNS overview and match to *Mathematics 5–14*

England: Match to NNS *Framework for teaching Mathematics* for Year 4

Strand	Topic	Teaching unit
Numbers and the number system	Place value, ordering and rounding	1, 2, 3, 13, 24, 25, 26, 27, 45, 46, 47
	Properties of numbers and number sequences	10, 11, 32, 50
	Fractions and decimals	18, 19, 20, 40, 41, 42, 43, 44, 54
Calculations	Understanding addition and subtraction	4, 21, 28
	Rapid recall of addition and subtraction facts	4, 34
	Mental calculation strategies (+ and −)	5, 6, 7, 8, 21, 28, 29, 33, 48, 55
	Pencil and paper procedures (+ and −)	8, 22, 30, 49
	Understanding multiplication and division	14, 36, 51
	Rapid recall of multiplication and division facts	12, 23
	Mental calculation strategies (× and ÷)	15, 37, 52
	Pencil and paper procedures (× and ÷)	16, 38, 53
	Checking results of calculations	4
Solving problems	Making decisions	9, 17
	Reasoning about numbers	35
	Problems involving 'real life', money or measures	9, 17, 31, 39

Scotland: Match to *Mathematics 5–14*, Levels B and C

	Strand	Level B	Level C	Teaching unit
Number, money and measurement	Range and type of numbers	Work with: – whole numbers up to 100 and then up to 1000 (count, order, read/write);	Work with: – whole numbers up to 1000 (count, order, read/write);	1, 2, 3, 25, 46
		– quarters (practical applications only).	– thirds, fifths, eighths, tenths and simple equivalences such as one half = two quarters (practical applications only); – decimals to two places when reading/recording money, and using calculator displays.	18, 19, 20, 40, 41 42, 43, 44, 54
	Money	Use coins up to £1 including exchange (50p = 5 × 10p).	Use coins/notes to £5 worth or more, including exchange.	9, 17, 36
	Add and subtract	Add and subtract: – mentally for numbers 0 to 20; in some cases beyond 20;	Add and subtract: – mentally for one digit to or from whole numbers up to three digits; beyond in some cases involving multiples of 10; – mentally for subtract on by 'adding on';	4, 5, 6, 7, 21, 28, 29, 33, 34, 48, 55
		– without a calculator for two-digit numbers – with a calculator for numbers to two digits added to or subtracted from three digits,	– without a calculator for whole numbers with two digits, added to or subtracted from three digits; – with a calculator for three-digit whole numbers,	8, 22, 30, 49
		in applications in number, measurement and money, including payments and change up to £1.	in applications in number, measurement and money to £20.	9, 17, 27, 31, 32, 39
	Multiply and divide	Multiply and divide: – mentally by 2, 3, 4, 5, 10, within the confines of these tables;	Multiply and divide: – mentally within the confines of all tables to 10; – mentally for any two- or three-digit whole number by 10;	12, 13, 14, 15, 23, 24, 35, 36, 37, 45, 50, 51, 52
		– without a calculator for two-digit numbers multiplied by 2, 3, 4, 5, 10; – with a calculator for two-digit numbers multiplied and divided by any digit,	– without a calculator for two-digit whole numbers by any single-digit whole number; – with a calculator for two- or three-digit whole numbers by a whole number with one or two digits;	16, 38, 53
		in applications in number, measurement and money to £1.	in applications in number, measurement and money to £20.	17, 31, 36, 39
	Round numbers	Round two-digit whole numbers to the nearest ten.	Round three-digit whole numbers to the nearest ten (e.g. when estimating).	26, 47
	Fractions, percentages and ratio	Find halves and quarters of quantities involving single- or two-digit numbers, for example by sharing.	Find simple fractions ($\frac{1}{3}, \frac{1}{5}, \frac{1}{10}$) of quantities involving single- or two-digit numbers.	18, 19, 20, 40, 41, 54
	Patterns and sequences	Work with patterns and sequences: – even and odd numbers; – whole number sequences within 100 (e.g. 10, 15, 20…, or 89, 79, 69…).	Work with patterns and relationships: – within and among multiplication tables.	5, 10, 11, 32, 35, 50
	Functions and equations	Find the missing numbers in statements where symbols are used for unknown numbers or operators.	Use a simple 'function machine' for operations: – involving doubling, halving, adding and subtracting.	15

Place value, ordering, rounding

Objectives

Read and write whole numbers to 10 000 in figures and in words.
Know what each digit represents.

Resources

- place-value cards
- slips of paper, each showing a two- or three-digit number
- box or bag for slips of paper
- 4 × 4 grid of four-digit numbers

What children are learning

- to read and write whole numbers from 0 to 10 000 in figures and words
- to partition numbers

Words you can use

number names from zero to ten thousand, thousands, hundreds, tens, units, ones,
number, digit, place value, partition

Things to note

- The activity begins with revision of reading whole numbers to 1000 before moving on
  to those to 10 000. It is important that children are confident with numbers up to
  1000 before moving on.
- Children often have difficulty writing three-digit numbers that have a zero in the tens
  column, for example 507, 809 etc. They may need extra help in creating these with
  place-value cards.

507   5 0 7

- Similarly, reading and writing four-digit numbers that have a zero in either the
  hundreds or tens column, for example 2804, 3051, can present difficulty, as can
  numbers with a zero in both these columns, for example 6004.
- Children often make mistakes when writing large numbers because they try to write
  what they hear, so to write three thousand, two hundred and sixty-four they may
  write 3000264.

Activities

❶ Read numbers from 0 to 1000 in figures and words.

- Give each child a set of place-value cards to 999 (i.e. numbers 1–9; multiples of 10 to 90; multiples of 100 to 900). Cut out several slips of paper and on each write a two- or three-digit number. Fold the slips and place them in a box or bag. Ask a child to take a piece of paper from the box and to read the number aloud, for example *three hundred and sixty-one.* Each child then makes the number using place-value cards.

  Have we all made the same number? Which cards did you use to make it? Repeat several times until children are confident with reading and making numbers to 1000. Explain that this process is called partitioning the number, for example 465 is partitioned into 400 + 60 + 5.

❷ Read and write numbers from 0 to 10 000 in figures and words.

- Make a 4 × 4 grid of four-digit numbers and give a copy to each child. They each choose and circle five numbers. They then take turns to pick one of the numbers from their grid and say it aloud. All children make the number using place-value cards. *How did you partition the number? Have you all made the same number?* Anyone who has that number circled on their grid can now cross if off, except for the child who chose the number. The winner is the first to cross off all five of their circled numbers.

- Say a number between 0 and 1000, for example *six hundred and twenty-three.* Children should write the number both in figures, as 623, and in words, as six hundred and twenty-three. Children can take turns to say a number within this range for the other children to record.

Feedback

Can each child:

- read and write whole numbers from 0 to 1000 in figures and in words?
- read and write whole numbers from 0 to 10 000 in figures and in words?

Which children can correctly read/write numbers with zeros in the hundreds, tens, or both columns?

Can each child correctly partition any four-digit number?

2 Place value, ordering, rounding

Objective

Know what each digit represents and partition into Th H T U.

Resources

▸ place-value cards for four-digit numbers
▸ calculators
▸ selection of four-digit number cards

What children are learning

▸ the value of each digit in numbers such as 3829
▸ how our number system works as we group units into tens, so 25 means 'two groups of 10 and 5 units' and as we group tens into hundreds and hundreds into thousands
▸ to partition (split) a four-digit number into thousands, hundreds, tens and units

Words you can use

hundreds, tens, units, ones, number, partition

Things to note

▸ Children need to be able to split, or partition, a number like 2453 into thousands, hundreds, tens and units, as in 'two thousands, four hundreds, five tens and three units' but they also need to appreciate the size of the number as a whole. Partitioning into 2000 + 400 + 50 + 3 as well as into 'two thousands, four hundreds, five tens and three units' can help children to see both the value of each column and the number as a whole.
▸ The idea that the position of a digit in a number determines its worth is known as 'place value'. Place value in our number system allows us to create an infinite series of numbers using just ten digits (0, 1, 2, 3, 4, 5, 6, 7, 8 and 9). Place-value cards can help children to appreciate that the 1 in the number 17 is worth ten etc.
▸ Children need to understand the role of 0 in a number. Zero is known as a 'place holder' and shows that there is an empty column, for example the 5 in 50 is worth five tens. Without 0, we would be unable to show the difference between 5, 50, 500, 5000, 50 000 etc. It can take children a long time to understand fully our system of writing numbers. Realizing the role of 0 is part of this understanding.

Activities

❶ Understand four-digit numbers.

▸ Each pair of children will need a set of place-value cards for four-digit numbers and a calculator. Player 1 picks four cards – thousands, hundreds, tens and units – and shows them to their partner. Player 2 keys into the calculator the number that these cards will make when combined. The number is checked by putting the place-value cards together. Player 2 wins a counter if they were right, and the two players swap roles.

▸ Again working in pairs, children pick a four-digit number card and key the number into the calculator. Player 1 writes down the number but changing one digit. Player 2 has to enter the correct addition/subtraction into the calculator so that the display changes to show the number that Player 1 has written down. For example, the chosen card shows 3241. Player 1 writes down 3741 so Player 2 needs to key $(+)(5)(0)(0)(=)$ into the calculator so that the display changes to 3741. Player 2 gets a point for doing this correctly, and the two players swap roles.

▸ If children are finding this work difficult, ask them to pick four numbers from a set of 0–9 cards and to combine them to make a four-digit number, for example 5297. Ask the children to say the number and then use place-value cards to make it. Emphasize that the left-hand digit is worth, in this case, five thousands (or 5000), the next digit is worth two hundreds (or 200), the next nine tens (or 90) and the right-hand digit is worth seven units.

Feedback

Can each child:

▸ identify what each digit in a four-digit number represents?
▸ partition a four-digit number into thousands, hundreds, tens and units?

If you point to a particular digit in a four-digit number, can each child tell you its value?

Who can tell you what the column to the left of the thousands will be? (Children frequently think it will be millions.)

Does each child know how many units are equal to a ten, how many tens make one hundred etc?

Objectives

Read and write the vocabulary of estimation.
Estimate up to 250 objects.

Resources

- containers holding up to 250 small items, for example 85 pasta shells, 157 beads etc.
- counters

What children are learning

- to gain an idea of how many things there are without counting, which helps to develop a 'feel' for numbers
- that an estimate doesn't need to be exact, but, instead, just needs to give a reasonable idea of the actual number

Words you can use

estimate, think, guess, nearly, about, close to, more than, less than, roughly, approximately, approximate

Things to note

- Emphasize that an estimate doesn't have to give the exact number, it is more of a 'good guess' to get a sense of how many there are. If children think they have to be 'spot on' they can be reluctant to estimate, preferring to count first and then pretend to have estimated the exact number.
- When estimating, people sometimes get clues from the arrangement of the objects, for example knowing that there are nine in the first arrangement and therefore that there are eighteen in the second. Looking for patterns of this type can help in

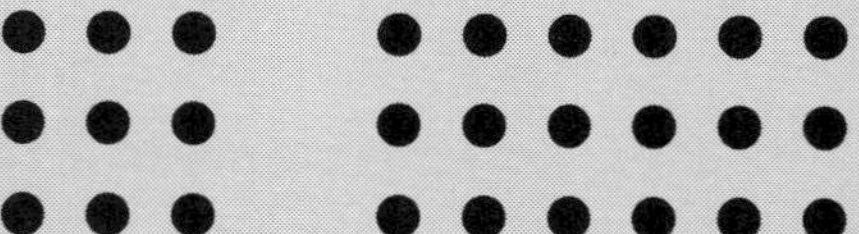

making a good estimate.
- Estimation activities are intended to help children improve their estimation skills. Children need to make their estimate on the basis of previous experience, for example 'There were thirty marbles in that pot but this pot is a bit bigger so I think it contains about forty marbles'.

Activities

❶ Read and write vocabulary of estimation. Estimate up to 250 objects

- ▸ Play this game as a group. Choose a container, tip out the contents and ask children to estimate the range. Record their estimates and then count the contents together. Children get a counter if the range they estimated is correct; the child who gives the narrowest range wins three counters.
- ▸ Children work individually, choosing a container and tipping out the contents. Instead of giving an estimate as a single number, encourage them to give a range within which the actual number falls. They could write, for example, 'between 140 and 200' or 'more than 150 but less than 200'. They then count the items and record the total on paper. If the actual number falls within their range they can win a counter or draw a counter next to their statement.

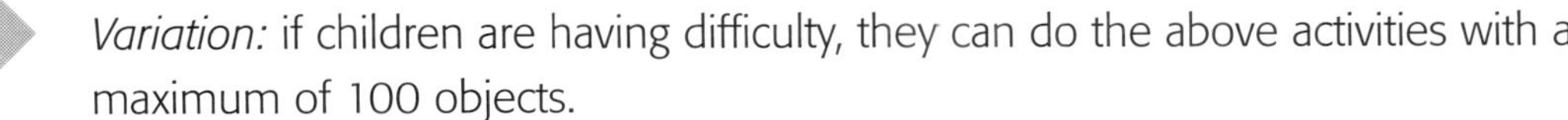

- ▸ As children improve their estimating ability they can be challenged to suggest a narrower range, for example between 150 and 180.
- ▸ Repeat the group activity, asking children to estimate the number of words on a page of a book. Demonstrate the strategy of getting an idea of the number of words in a line, for example ten, and estimating the number of lines on the page as a way of getting a reasonable estimate.
- ▸ *Variation:* if children are having difficulty, they can do the above activities with a maximum of 100 objects.

Feedback

Can each child:
- ▸ give a sensible estimate of up to 250 objects?
- ▸ explain why they have given a certain estimate on the basis of past experience?

Does any child continue to give almost random guesses?

Are children happy to estimate, or are they over-concerned about not getting the exact answer, or giving a 'wrong' answer?

Rapid recall of number facts (+ and –)/ Understanding addition and subtraction

Objectives

Consolidate knowing by heart all addition and subtraction facts for each number up to 20.
Consolidate understanding of relationship between addition and subtraction.
Understand commutative law of addition.
Check with addition in a different order.

Resources

- 0–10 number cards
- 0–20 number line

What children are learning

- to recall or derive quickly answers to addition and subtraction questions for numbers up to 20
- to appreciate that addition is the inverse of subtraction, and vice versa (i.e. that subtraction 'undoes' addition, and vice versa)
- that two numbers can be added in any order, and to use this for checking answers

Words you can use

add, sum, total, altogether, plus, and, more, make, take away, minus, subtract, less than, leaves, equals, increase by, decrease by, difference between

Things to note

- You may need to remind children to think carefully about the order of the numbers in subtraction questions because, unlike addition, subtraction cannot be done in any order.
- The vocabulary for subtraction can be confusing. Help children to explain a calculation in a useful way such as 'You are starting with ten and then working out what number is three fewer'.
- Older children who were introduced to the = sign as an 'answer' sign sometimes struggle with the = sign in equations such as $3 + 2 = 4 + 1$ where there are two numbers to the right ($3 + 2$ does not equal 4). It is therefore important to introduce the = sign to mean 'is the same as' or 'is equal to' rather than 'gives the answer', to avoid confusion later.
- The term 'number sentence' is used to describe an equation which includes numbers, an operation sign ($+$, $-$, $\times$ or $\div$), an = sign and an answer. These are all number sentences: $\qquad 3 + 2 = 5 \qquad 23 - 20 = 3 \qquad 4 \times 5 = 20$

Activities

❶ Consolidate knowledge of addition and subtraction facts for numbers to 20.

- Begin by giving each pair of children a set of 0–10 number cards and asking them to take turns to turn over two cards, add them and say the number sentence, for example 'six plus nine equals fifteen'. Encourage children to use addition strategies if they do not 'know' the number fact, for example bridging through 10 or adding 10 and subtracting 1. Children should then record the fact on paper. When children have written a range of addition facts they can check each other's answers. Suggest that the checking could be done using a different method.

- As a group, ask the children to follow simple number chains, for example *Start with the number ten, add five, subtract ten, add four, add nine. Which number do you end on?* (18) Ensure children have time to follow each stage of the number chain and provide questions where numbers do not cross the 20 boundary. Vary the vocabulary to include words like 'plus', 'more', 'take away', 'minus', 'subtract', 'less'; introduce the words 'increase by', 'decrease by'. Invite a child to track the number chain on a 0–20 number line and emphasize that addition involves moving in one direction on the line, and subtraction involves moving in the other direction. *If I add seven, what could I do to 'undo' that?* (subtract 7)

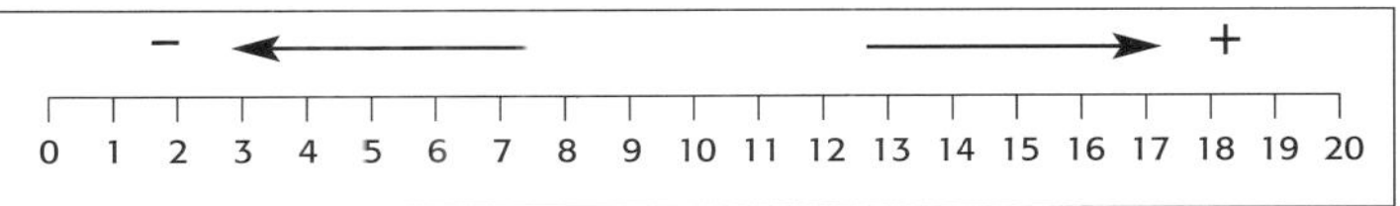

- Children can then write their own number chains. Stress that the chain should never go above 20 (this will ensure that children work out their own number chains as they write them). Ask children to swap papers or to read out their chains for the group to work out. Provide number lines for children who might benefit from counting forwards and backwards to follow the number chains.

Feedback

Can each child recall or derive quickly answers to addition and subtraction questions for numbers up to 20?

Does each child:
- appreciate that addition is the inverse of subtraction, and vice versa?
- use the fact that two numbers can be added in any order to check their answers?

Which facts are children unsure of?

Which strategies do children use to work out unknown facts?

Is anyone reliant on counting on/back in ones as their main strategy?

5 Mental calculation strategies (+ and –)

Objective
Count on or back in repeated steps of 1, 10 and 100.

Resources
▸ cards made from **PCM 1**

What children are learning
▸ to count on or back in steps of 1, 10 or 100 to numbers between 0 and 10 000
▸ to use the patterns in our number system to help with counting and calculating
▸ to use these skills to find answers to addition and subtraction questions

Words you can use
digit, tens, units, hundreds, thousands, number, add, sum, total, altogether, plus, and, more, make, take away, minus, subtract, less than, leaves, equals, increase by, decrease by

Things to note
▸ The ability to add/subtract 1, 10 or 100 to or from any number relies on an appreciation of place value. Place value is the idea that the position of a digit in a number determines its worth, for example the 4 in 42 stands for four tens or 40 whereas the 4 in 420 stands for four hundreds or 400. Place value in our number system allows us to create an infinite series of numbers using just ten digits (0, 1, 2, 3, 4, 5, 6, 7, 8 and 9).
▸ Place-value cards are particularly useful in helping children to appreciate the differences between the digits in two- and three-digit numbers, for example 342 can be shown as 300 + 40 + 2.
▸ Children may have particular difficulty in counting through boundary values – multiples of 100 or 1000, for example the next ten after 3297. (Specific practice of this is given in teaching unit 7.)

Activities
❶ **Count on or back in repeated steps of 1, 10 or 100.**
▸ Ask a variety of questions that involve counting on or back in steps of 1, 10 or 100, for example *Count on from 165 in tens. Count back in ones from 1004. Count back in hundreds from 843*. Write the start number on the board each time and ask questions about the digits, for example *How many units in this number? How many tens? How many hundreds? How many thousands?* Either count in unison or ask children to sit in a circle and count around the circle, with each child saying the next number.

▸ If children have difficulty with this, write the numbers in each pattern on the board and discuss which of the digits changes, revising place value for thousands, hundreds, tens and units. If children have particular problems at boundaries, model the count using base-10 apparatus. Invite a child to exchange ten tens for a hundred, or ten hundreds for a thousand. Show the equivalent change in the written number.

▸ Play this game using cards made from **PCM 1**, shuffled and placed face down on the table. Write a three- or four-digit start number above 700 on the board or on a large piece of paper. Ask a child to pick a card. Explain to the children that they should start with the number written on the board and try to follow the instruction on the card by counting on or back in steps of 1, 10 or 100. For example, the card marked 'minus 600' would be worked out by counting back in six steps of a hundred. Assist children with the vocabulary used where necessary.

Compare answers. Invite a child to explain/demonstrate how they got the answer. If necessary, count together. Repeat with other start numbers and cards.

Feedback

Can each child:

▸ count on or back in steps of 1, 10 or 100 to numbers between 0 and 10 000?
▸ use these skills to find answers to addition and subtraction questions?

Does each child:

▸ appreciate place value for thousands, hundreds, tens and units (ones)?
▸ know how many units make one ten, how many tens make one hundred etc?

Who could count correctly in tens or hundreds through boundary numbers?

Mental calculation strategies (+ and –)

Objectives

Derive doubles of whole numbers to 50 and corresponding halves.
Identify near doubles.

Resources

- 1–30 number cards

What children are learning

to use their knowledge of doubles of numbers to 30 as a basis for finding further
number facts

Words you can use

double, twice, near, add, plus, sum, makes, equals

Things to note

- 'Near doubles' are pairs of consecutive numbers being added together, for example
  15 and 16. Children can use their knowledge of doubles to find 'near doubles', for
  example to find 15 + 16, children might know that double 15 is 30 so 15 + 16 is one
  more than 30, = 31.
- Children will be able to make use of this particular strategy only if they are familiar
  with doubles of numbers. This lesson includes revision of doubles to 30. A list of the
  doubles to 30 could be written and used as a guide for children who have difficulty
  remembering the facts. Later work can extend this lesson to include doubles to 50.
- To work out doubles quickly, children will need to be confident with partitioning and
  then recombining numbers. For example, to work out double 46: double 40 is 80,
  double 6 is 12, so double 46 is 80 + 12, which is 92.

Activities

❶ Revise doubles of whole numbers to 30.

- Children pick a 1–30 number card, for example 15, and
  state the number's double, saying 'double 15 is 30' or
  'twice 15 is 30'. Continue until the doubles of all the
  numbers from 1 to 30 have been revised. *How many is
  double sixteen? What is twice thirteen?*
- Play Bingo as a group. Children write down five even numbers from 2 to 60. Call
  out numbers from 1 to 30 for children to double. They cross off the answer if they
  have it, and call 'Bingo!' when they have crossed off all five numbers. Keep a note
  of the numbers you have called so that you can check they are correct.

❷ Derive unknown doubles of numbers to 50.
On the board demonstrate the strategy of splitting numbers
into tens and units and then doubling each part separately.
Explain that this method can be used to find doubles that
they don't yet know. Invite children to work through examples
on the board.

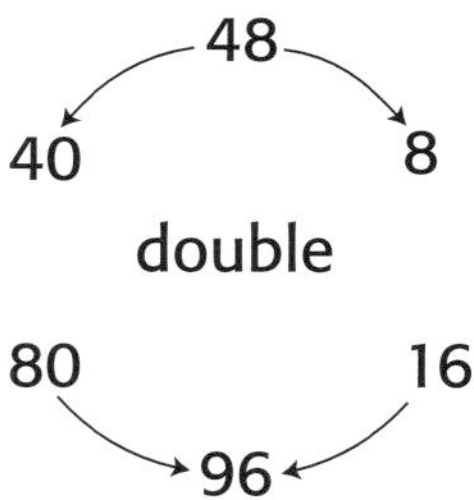

❸ Identify near doubles using doubles already known.

▸ Turn over two consecutive number cards, for example 15 and 16. Cover the 16
with your finger or a counter. *Can anyone tell me what double fifteen is?* Uncover
the 16. *How many more is this than fifteen? Double fifteen is thirty. The question
is fifteen plus sixteen. We know that sixteen is one more than fifteen, so the
answer must be one more than double fifteen, which is one more than thirty,
making thirty-one.*

▸ Repeat for 16 + 17, encouraging the children to see the sum 16 + 17 as adding 1
more to double 16, which they already know. Solve these questions in the same
way: 14 + 15, 17 + 18, 20 +21, 18 + 19, 19 + 20, 22 + 23, 25 + 26 etc.

▸ Introduce questions where the second number is one less, for example 17 + 16.
How can we find the answer to this? Explain that this can be solved by doubling
17 and finding one less, or by doubling 16 and finding one more.

Variation: children can find near doubles of numbers up to 50.

Feedback

Can each child:

▸ recall the doubles of numbers to 30?
▸ explain a method for working out doubles of numbers to 50?
▸ identify near doubles, using doubles of numbers to 50?

Does anyone have difficulty doubling numbers that have a units digit of 5 or more?

Mental calculation strategies (+ and −)

Objective

Count up through next multiple of 10, 100, 1000.

Resources

- digit strips and frame made from **PCM 2**
- number lines

What children are learning

- to count up in ones and tens through multiples of 10, 100 or 1000, for example count on seven from 38, 297 or 3999 etc.
- to appreciate how our number system works, that numbers are grouped into tens so that one more than nine units makes an extra ten and no units, for example $89 + 1 = 90$. Where there are already nine tens, the hundreds digit also changes as one more is added, for example $399 + 1 = 400$

Words you can use

number, count on, hundreds, thousands, tens, units, digit, more, add, difference, plus

Things to note

- Sections of number line, for example from 90 to 110, can provide a useful means of exploring the numbers either side of a tens, hundreds or thousands boundary. Counting on using such a line can give children confidence or can be used to check answers.
- If children are unsure of counting over a boundary, model the count using base-10 apparatus, exchanging ten ones for one ten; ten tens for one hundred etc. Compare this with the corresponding count written in figures.

Activities

❶ Count up through the next multiple of 10, 100 or 1000.

- Attach the four 0–9 number strips to the rectangular frame from **PCM 2** to show 77. *What number does this show? What number would be one more than this?* Move the units digits to show 78. *What if we added one hundred to this number?* Move the hundreds digit to show 178. Move the hundreds digit back one to show 78 again. *What have we subtracted? If we count on in steps of one, what happens?* Demonstrate changing the strips to show 78, 79 … *What happens now?*

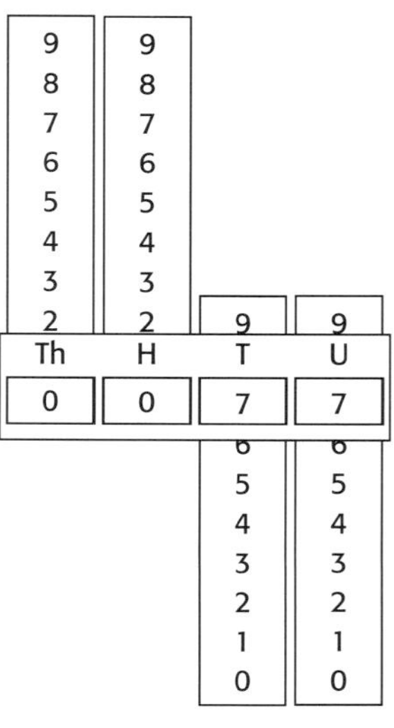

Discuss that the number after 79 is 80. *If a number has nine units, and we add one more unit, we can't have ten units in this column so the ten units become one more ten in the tens column.* Continue counting in ones up to 89 and demonstrate the changeover at the 90 boundary. Keep counting in ones up to 99 and demonstrate changing the units, tens and hundreds columns to make 100.

- Now change the start number to 686. *What number is this? How many hundreds has this number? How many tens/units?* Ask the children to count on in ones up to 700 and beyond. Use the place-value strips to demonstrate how the numbers change at the 690 and 700 boundaries. Ask children to record the numbers in a sequence, for example 686, 687, 688, 689, 690, 691 …
- Change the start number to 2987. *What number is this? How many hundreds/ tens/units/thousands has this number?* Ask the children to count on in ones up to 3000 and beyond. Demonstrate the changes at the 2990 and 3000 boundaries. Again, ask children to record the numbers and repeat for other numbers that are just below a tens, hundreds or thousands boundary.
- *Variations:* ask children to count on a particular number of steps in ones, for example 'count on seven steps of one from 896' and record this as an addition: 896 + 7 = 903. Alternatively, use this as a means of exploring differences, for example 903 − 896 = 7.
- The activities can be repeated for counting on in tens. Remind the children that when counting on in tens, the units digit does not change.

Feedback

Can each child count up in ones through multiples of 10, 100 and 1000?

Does each child know how many ones make one ten, how many tens make one hundred etc?

Is everyone confident using base-10 apparatus to model adding one to 399, for example exchanging ten units for one ten, and then ten tens for one hundred?

Mental calculation strategies (+ and –)/ Pencil and paper procedures (+ and –)

Objectives

Add/subtract a pair of two-digit numbers (not crossing 10 or 100 boundary). Use informal pencil and paper methods to support, record or explain addition and subtraction.

Resources

- 10–89 number cards
- counters

What children are learning

to use informal jottings to support, record or explain how they worked out the answer to an addition question

Words you can use

add, plus, sum, total, altogether, answer, method, tens, units

Things to note

- Children should be confident with adding numbers mentally before beginning to add numbers using a formal written method, for example setting out their work vertically in columns. The following activity can be carried out with children using mental methods. Children may need to use informal jottings to support their calculation.
- This unit focuses on adding pairs of two-digit numbers as this must be fully understood before tackling addition with larger numbers. Children need to be able to use a variety of methods.

Activities

❶ **Add pairs of two-digit numbers using mental methods (and informal jottings).**

- On the board write pairs of numbers that, when added, do not cross a tens boundary, for example 42 + 16, 37 + 32, 24 + 53. Draw attention to the fact that these are two-digit numbers, having a tens number and a units number. *How many tens has this number? How many units has it?* Remind children to bear this in mind when adding these pairs of numbers. Discuss the first pair of numbers and ask the children to find the total by adding them. (58) Describe this in different ways, using a range of vocabulary, for example *What is the sum of 43 and 25?*

What is the total? What is 43 plus 25? Ask children to work out the answer and to explain how they did it, for example 'I added 40 and 20 to make 60, and then added on 3 more to make 63 and then added 5 to make 68'.

‣ Invite children to write their method, for example:

$$40 + 20 = 60 \quad 60 + 3 = 63 \quad 63 + 5 = 68$$

Some children may use empty number lines to help them, for example:

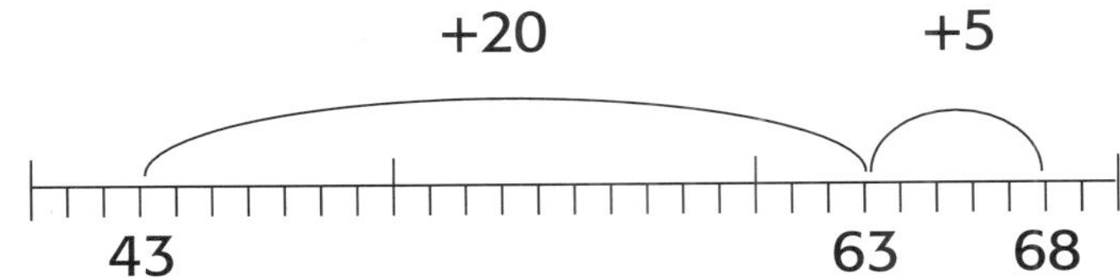

Discuss the different methods used. Children will use different methods to answer the same question; encourage them to use the method that they find easiest. The methods used will vary for different calculations, for example to answer 62 + 19, many children will add 20 then subtract 1.

‣ Continue in the same way, discussing different methods used by the children.

❷ **Pairs game.**
Give each pair a pile of 10–89 numbers cards. Each child takes two cards and adds the numbers together. The child with the bigger total wins a counter. Can they predict before they add who will have the bigger total? Encourage children to jot down how they worked out the calculation so that their partner can check.

Feedback

Can each child:

‣ use jottings to support, record or explain how they worked out mentally the answer to an addition question?
‣ add mentally pairs of two-digit numbers?

What methods do children use for their mental additions?

Is anyone reliant on counting on in ones?

9 Money and 'real-life' problems/ Making decisions, checking results

Objectives

Convert £ to p.
Choose appropriate number operations and calculation methods to solve money or real-life word problems with one step.

Resources

▸ a page from a catalogue or a price list with prices less than £20 given in pounds, for example £13·45, £4·99, £7·05 – one copy for each child
▸ cards made from **PCM 3**

What children are learning

▸ to convert amounts of money in pounds to pence, for example £1·25 = 125p
▸ to decide what to do and how to solve real-life problems involving money

Words you can use

sort, set, coins, 1p, 2p, 5p, 10p, 20p, 50p, £1, £2, £5 note, £10 note, coins, pound, pence, penny, how many?, total, cost, pay, price, count, number, more, fewer, altogether, left, subtract, change, answer, total, solve, problem, add, subtract, multiply, divide, method, record, cost, value, change

Things to note

▸ Never use both a pound sign and a pence sign when recording an amount. If a decimal point is used it should be in conjunction with the pound sign only, for example £5·24 (never £5·24p).
▸ Children often find it difficult to decide whether to add, subtract, multiply or divide when solving worded problems. Avoid just telling them what to do. Encourage other children to explain the problem in their own words and to record the method using informal jottings. At this stage children are not expected to set out questions in a formal way, for example using vertical columns. Instead children should be encouraged to write horizontally, using notation they are comfortable with.
▸ These activities focus on exploring the *methods* used to solve a problem; working out the calculation to find the answer is secondary. Accordingly, problems should not involve difficult numbers so that children are not distracted.

Activities

❶ Convert £ to p.

▸ Give each child a page from a catalogue or a price list (see above), or write some prices in pounds on a large piece of paper, for example video, £12·75; book, £3·99. Ask questions about the prices, for example *Jenny, how much is the tape recorder? What is the price of the personal stereo? What does the cartoon video cost? How many pounds is the book?* Emphasize the word 'pound' as answers are given and explain that we say that these prices are 'in pounds'. Hold up a £1 coin and a 1p coin. *How many one-pence pieces are the same as one pound?* Remind children that there are 100 pence in a pound. Write 'In pounds' and 'In pence' on the board and write some prices beneath the 'In pounds' heading. *Prices can be given in pounds or in pence.* Encourage children to suggest how the prices in pounds could be given as prices in pence, for example £1·40 = 140p.

In pounds	In pence
£1·40	140p
£3·75	
£12·99	

▸ Ask children to rewrite the prices from the catalogue or price list in pence rather than in pounds. Remind children that they will not need to use a decimal point.

❷ Decide how to solve money or real-life word problems.
Choose one of the problem cards made from **PCM 3**. Read the problem together and discuss it using a mixture of vocabulary to create a picture of what the problem is about. Discuss methods to solve the problem, asking individual children *how* they would find the answer. Encourage children to explain their thinking to each other and, if necessary, to use jottings to do any working. Discuss the answers and methods, for example *What would you do to find the answer? Which numbers would you use? Which method of addition/subtraction/ multiplication/division would you use?* Discuss other cards from the PCM, inviting individual children to explain the problem and how they would tackle it.

Feedback

Can each child:

▸ convert amounts of money in pounds to pence, for example £1·25 = 125p?
▸ convert an amount with a zero in the tens column, for example £3·05 = 305p?
▸ decide what to do and how to solve real-life problems involving money?

Does anyone have difficulty identifying which operation to use to solve a one-step problem?

10 Numbers and number sequences

Objective

Recognize and extend number sequences formed by counting from any number in steps of constant size, for example 25 to 500.

Resources

- number line
- copy of **PCM 4** for each child
- counters

What children are learning

- to count in steps of a constant size from any number
- to recognize, continue and explain number sequences

Words you can use

count on, steps, multiple, zero, number, sequence, pattern, difference, more, less, tens, units, predict, continue, rule

Things to note

- Counting forwards (and backwards) in different sized steps helps children to gain an understanding of how numbers relate to each other. Children build up a picture in their minds of where numbers are, and over time are able to visualize how many more or less a number is than another without needing to count. Counting on in steps of a constant size helps children to answer addition and subtraction questions without needing to count, for example 14 + 7 can be answered by *knowing* that seven more than fourteen is twenty-one. Counting on and back can also help children to recognize, continue and explain number sequences, for example 3, 7, 11, 15 …
- Once children can count on or back in steps of, for example two, three, four or five, they can begin to count in steps of multiples of 10 or 100 such as 20, 300, 40, 500 etc.
- To count in steps, children need a good understanding of how our number system works and the patterns in our number system. Using number lines/100 squares as models can help.

Activities

❶ **Count on in steps of a constant size from any number.**
- Before copying **PCM 4**, write the following numbers in the frogs of the first nine lines. (These can be simplified if too difficult for the children in the group.)
  2   20   5   50   3   300   4   400   25

These numbers give the size of the step that the children count on in. Write a small start number in the first lily pad of each line. Note how each pair of lines is related and ensure that the start numbers are also related in an appropriate way. For example, in lines one and two the children count on in twos and twenties, respectively, so the start numbers might be 4 and 40, respectively. Give each child a copy of the PCM and ask them to fill in the numbers on the lily-pad trails by counting on in steps of the size shown in each frog. Discuss the patterns that the children see. *What do you notice about counting on in twos and in twenties? Can you use this sequence to help you answer this one? How many times bigger than two is twenty? How many times bigger are the numbers in this sequence than the numbers in this one?* Ask the children to extend the sequences as far as they can. Some may need to use a 100 square or number line.

▸ Once the lily-pad trails have been filled in, ask children to check their answers in pairs by counting their numbers aloud. Any differences can be checked with the rest of the group. The numbers could be read backwards from the largest number to practise counting backwards in steps of a constant size.

▸ Children can then cover some of their numbers with counters. In pairs, children predict which numbers are hidden.

Variations: a large number, for example 150 or 200, can be written in the first lily pad and children can count back in steps of a constant size. Children can be given the first three numbers in a sequence and asked to work out the rule, fill in the step size on the frog and continue the sequence.

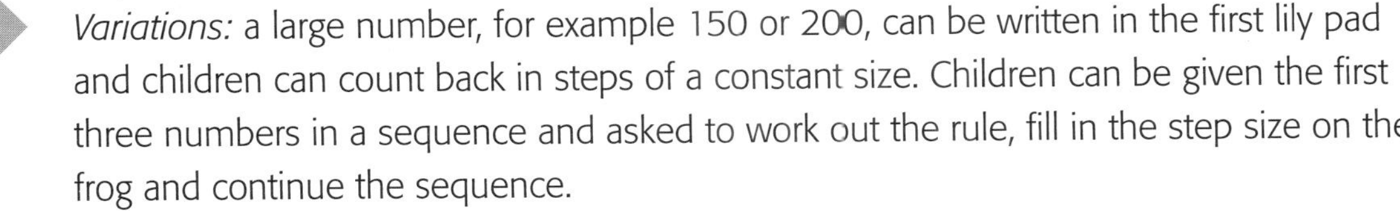

Feedback

Can each child:

▸ count in steps of a constant size from any number, for example 30, 400, 25 etc?
▸ recognize, continue and explain number sequences?

Did anyone need a number line or 100 square for support?

Which children commented on patterns in the sequence or used them to predict?

Numbers and number sequences

Objective

Recognize odd and even numbers up to 1000 and some of their properties, for example sums, differences of pairs of odd/even numbers.

Resources

▸ 10–99 number cards that children can write on

What children are learning

▸ to recognize odd and even numbers to 1000
▸ to understand that when adding and subtracting odd and even numbers, something can be predicted about the answer, for example it will be an odd answer

Words you can use

odd, even, count on, count back, twos, pairs, add, sum, total, plus, difference

Things to note

▸ It is important that children know that numbers with a units digit of 0, 2, 4, 6 or 8 are even numbers and that those ending with 1, 3, 5, 7 or 9 are odd numbers.
▸ The definition of an even number is one that can be divided equally into two whole number parts, for example 2 can be split into one and one without a remainder. Any number that is not even is an odd number.
▸ Note that properties of odd and even numbers include patterns that can be found when adding and subtracting.

even + even = even	odd + odd = even	even + odd = odd	odd + even = odd
even − even = even	odd − odd = even	even − odd = odd	odd − even = odd

Activities

❶ **Recognize odd and even numbers up to 1000.**

▸ Write the following numbers on the board: 37, 600, 94, 540 and 11. *Which of these numbers can we find half of?* Record underneath as shown. *Why is it difficult to find half of thirty-seven and half of eleven? Which numbers can be halved to give a whole number?* Circle these. *What is special about these numbers? These are even numbers. They are multiples of two. How do we recognize even numbers?* (They end in 0, 2, 4, 6 or 8.) Write some three-digit numbers on the board and invite children to circle the even numbers.

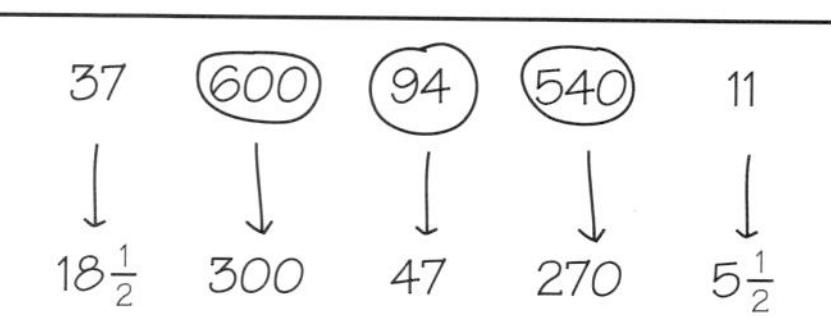

- Explain that a postman has to deliver letters to 'Long Lane'. The houses along one side of the street are the even numbers in order; the odd numbers are on the opposite side. The postman walks up the left-hand side of the street and then back down the other side. Ask questions such as *Which house will he go to after number 123? Before 139? Which houses does number 364 lie between? Can you tell me the next ten houses he goes to after number 189?* (Make sure that you say the numbers in full – 'one hundred and twenty-three' rather than 'one, two, three'.)

❷ Recognize properties of odd and even numbers.
Put the children in pairs, designating one as 'even' and one as 'odd'. They pick a 10–99 number card. If the number is even, the 'even' child takes the card and writes 'even' on the back. If the number on the card is odd, the 'odd' child takes the card and writes 'odd' on the back. Draw children's attention to the units digit in each number if they are unsure. Once all cards have been labelled, ask the children to choose any two even-number cards. *Add these two even numbers. Is the answer odd or even?* Invite children to suggest the answers, and write 'even + even = even' on the board, for example 24 + 58 = 82. *Is this always true? Try two different even cards and check.* Ask children to explore 'odd + odd = even' and 'even + odd = odd' in the same way. Ensure children realize that they must check with other examples before the rule is 'proved'.

▶ *Variation:* if appropriate, children can explore differences, for example even − even = even; odd − odd = even; even − odd = odd; odd − even = odd.

Feedback

Can each child:
- recognize odd and even numbers to 1000?
- understand that when adding and subtracting odd and even numbers, some information can be predicted about the answers?
- explain how they know that 943, for example, is an odd number?

Are children able to suggest a 'rule' about adding/subtracting odd/even numbers by trying out examples?

Rapid recall of number facts ($\times$ and $\div$)

Objective

Recall multiplication facts in the 2, 3, 4, 5, and 10 times tables and derive division facts.

Resources

- a set of playing cards with the picture cards removed
- 0–100 number cards

What children are learning

the multiplication facts for the 2, 3, 4, 5 and 10 times tables, together with the corresponding division facts, for example $5 \times 6 = 30$ and $30 \div 5 = 6$

Words you can use

times, lots of, multiplied by, multiply, share, divide, divided by

Things to note

- The learning of number facts is an ongoing process throughout the year. This lesson could be repeated several times during the year to provide practice and assessment of the addition facts children are required to learn.
- Some children have particular difficulty memorizing facts. Provide children with opportunities to see, feel, hear and say the number facts in a variety of ways. Use different 'voices' to read number facts aloud, for example whisper, shout, squeak etc. Ask children to use a finger to trace the facts in the air, on the table, on another child's back, into their own palm etc.
- Where children have difficulty remembering facts, encourage them to develop strategies to derive them quickly, for example to multiply a number by four you can double it and then double the answer.
- Describe multiplication questions using a range of vocabulary including 'times', 'multiplied by', 'lots of', 'groups of', 'sets of' and division questions using 'shared between', 'divided by' etc. Children should appreciate that once a multiplication fact is known, so are corresponding division facts, for example $3 \times 5 = 15$, $15 \div 3 = 5$ etc.

Activities

❶ Recall multiplication facts for the 2, 3, 4, 5 and 10 times tables.

- On a piece of paper, draw five playing-card outlines and next to them write $\times 2 =$, $\times 3 =$, $\times 4 =$, $\times 5 =$ and $\times 10 =$.

$\boxed{}\ \times 2 = \quad \boxed{}\ \times 3 = \quad \boxed{}\ \times 4 = \quad \boxed{}\ \times 5 = \quad \boxed{}\ \times 10 =$

Shuffle the playing cards. Deal five cards onto the outlines to create a series of multiplication questions, for example $4 \times 2 =$, $5 \times 3 =$, $8 \times 4 =$, $7 \times 5 =$, $5 \times 10 =$. Ask a child to read each question and say the answer, for example 'four times two equals eight' or 'four multiplied by two is eight'. If correct they win a counter. If any of the answers are the same, the child wins a bonus counter. Repeat for the next child. Encourage the others to say whether the answers are correct.

▶ *Variation:* ask the children to write down the questions and the answers. Give them time to do this and then award a point to all those with the correct answer. Encourage the children to use vocabulary of multiplication – times, lots of, multiplied by etc.

▸ If children are having difficulty remembering the number facts for a particular table, use the following activity. Draw an eleven-box number track and lay number cards for the 3 times table (0, 3, 6, 9 … 30), for example, in order, face down in the boxes. *We are going to count up in threes. What is zero times three?* Turn over the 0-card. *What is ten times three?* Turn over the 30-card. *What goes in the middle? How many lots of three is this? What other multiples of three do we know? How?* Encourage children to use facts they know to work out unknown facts, for example if you know $2 \times 3 = 6$, then you can double it to get $4 \times 3 = 12$. If you know $5 \times 3 = 15$, then you can work out that $6 \times 3 = 18$, which is three more. Once all the cards are turned over, count in unison forwards and backwards along the track. Turn some of the cards face down and repeat.

❷ Derive division facts for the 2, 3, 4, 5 and 10 times tables.

▸ Repeat the first activity, asking children to write down a corresponding division fact for each question generated, for example $4 \times 2 = 8$ gives $8 \div 4 = 2$. Encourage the children to use vocabulary of division – share, divide, divided by etc.

▸ Set up a times table number line, as in the second activity above, and turn all the cards face up. *How many threes make twenty-one?* With the children count up: *No threes are zero, one three is three, two threes are six, three threes are nine…* to find the answer. Explain that this can be used to work out the answer to $21 \div 3$. *How can we work out twenty-seven divided by three?*

Feedback

Can each child:

▸ recall multiplication facts for the 2, 3, 4, 5 and 10 times tables?

▸ use doubling to work out the two times table?

▸ derive corresponding division facts?

Which facts are children confident about?

Can everyone work out facts that they can't remember, for example working out a 4 times table fact by doubling and doubling again?

Does everyone realize that $\square \times 0 = 0$?

Objective

Multiply whole numbers by 10 (and 100).

Resources

- 0–100 number cards
- several sets of 0–9 number cards
- Blu-tack
- calculators

What children are learning

- to multiply a number by 10 we move the digits one place to the left and fill the space with a zero, for example:

H	T	U	
	4	5	× 10
4	5	0	

- to multiply by 100 we move the digits two places to the left

Words you can use

multiply, ten, hundred, digit, place value

Things to note

- Avoid telling children to 'add a zero' when multiplying by 10. This works only for whole numbers and causes confusion when children meet decimals, for example 8·6 × 10 = 86, not 8·60. Instead, focus attention on moving the digits one place to the left when multiplying by 10 and two places to the left when multiplying by 100.
- Children may find it helpful to physically move digits, for example through using a place-value board with digit cards.

Activities

❶ **To multiply by 10, shift the digits one place to the left.**

- Write the column headings 'H' 'T' 'U' on the board and Blu-tack an 8-card in the units column. *What is this number worth?* Key in 8 on the calculator and show it to the children. *What will happen to this number if I multiply it by 10?* Key in (×) (1) (0) (=) and ask a child to record the answer on the board by moving the 8-card into the tens column and putting a 0-card in the units column.

Repeat the process for other single-digit numbers, inviting different children to move the cards on the board. *What do you notice about the numbers we have multiplied by ten? What has happened to each of them?* Emphasize that each has moved one place to the left, and a zero has filled in the gap left in the units column.

- Stick number cards to show 15 in the table, and enter 15 in the calculator. *What do you think the answer will be if we multiply fifteen by ten?* Confirm the suggestions on the calculator and invite a child to move the cards one column to the left and add a zero to make 150 in the table. *What about eighteen multiplied by ten? Thirty-four multiplied by ten?* Invite different children to move the cards. *What is happening each time?*

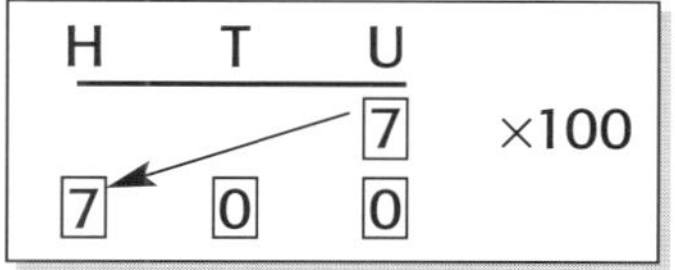

- Give children a calculator and ask them to choose a number from a set of 0–100 cards and to predict the answer if we multiply by 10. Record the chosen number and the answer in a table. Alternatively, children could use place-value tables and digit cards.

❷ To multiply by 100, shift the digits two places to the left.

- If children are ready, move on to multiplying by 100. *What do you think will happen if we multiply by 100?* Write a new H T U table on the board and Blu-tack a 7-card in the units column. *What happens to the seven if we multiply by one hundred?* Demonstrate how the 7 moves two places to the left. Repeat for several single-digit numbers.

- Introduce multiplying two-digit numbers by 100 in the same way.

- Draw the plan shown on the board. Explain that this is a plan of the hall. The scale of the map is 1:100. This means that whatever the length an object is drawn on the plan, it is actually 100 times bigger in real life. Ask questions such as *How long is the hall in real life?* Ask children to draw objects of their own, marking the plan length and the real-life length.

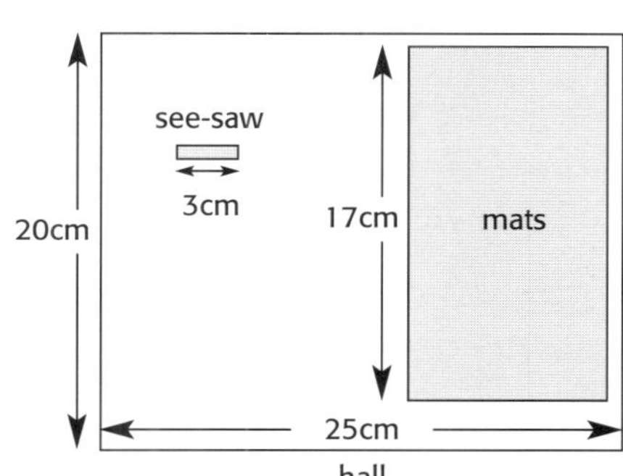

Feedback

Can each child:
- multiply by 10?
- multiply by 100?
- read calculator displays?

Are children able to tell you the value of each column?

14 Understanding multiplication and division

Objective

Extend understanding of multiplication and division and their relationship to each other.

Resources

- cubes or counters
- 0–10 number cards
- blank cards

What children are learning

- that multiplication is the opposite, or inverse, of division, and vice versa
- that each division statement has a matching multiplication statement that will 'undo' it, for example $20 \div 5 = 4$ and $4 \times 5 = 20$
- that multiplication questions can be checked through division, and vice versa

Words you can use

multiply, times, lots of, divide, share, makes, equals

Things to note

- Children should realize that multiplication is the opposite, or inverse, of division, and vice versa. This means we can 'undo' multiplication with division, and vice versa, so $4 \times 3 = 12$ and $12 \div 4 = 3$ etc.
- It is also important that children realize that if we know one number sentence we can work out three more, for example from $4 \times 3 = 12$ we can create the multiplication sentence $3 \times 4 = 12$ and the division sentences $12 \div 4 = 3$ and $12 \div 3 = 4$.
- We often answer a division question by using our knowledge of multiplication, for example we answer $16 \div 8$ by thinking 'how many eights make sixteen?'

Activities

❶ **Extend understanding of multiplication and division and their relationship to each other.**
- Ask multiplication and related division questions set in a real-life context. *How many wheels on a car?* (4) *If there are three cars, how many wheels is that?* (12) (Children can sketch this if necessary.) *How can we write this as a multiplication sum?* ($4 \times 3 = 12$) *If I had a stack of thirty-two wheels to put on cars, how many cars will that be?* (8) *What division calculation describes this?* ($32 \div 4 = 8$)

Encourage children to write their own stories and the number sentences, for example 'There are five cars that need new tyres. This makes twenty tyres altogether.' ($5 \times 4 = 20$) 'There are twenty tyres in the pile. That's enough for five cars.' ($20 \div 4 = 5$)

▸ On the board write multiplication sentences with an equivalent division sentence elsewhere on the board, for example:

   $6 \times 4 = 24$ $4 \times 3 = 12$ $2 \times 9 = 18$ $24 \div 6 = 4$

   $18 \div 2 = 9$ $7 \times 4 = 28$ $28 \div 4 = 7$ $12 \div 4 = 3$

All these sentences have a partner. Can you join up the pairs of statements? Why did you join those?

▸ Children choose two from a set of 0–10 number cards, for example 4 and 6. (Children can use 0–5 or 0–6 number cards, if necessary.) They arrange these to make a multiplication sentence, work out the answer and write the answer on a blank card. They write the sentence in their books and then rearrange the cards to create a division sentence using the same numbers, as shown, which they record underneath. *Can you write another division sentence using the same numbers?*

6	×	4	=	24
24	÷	6	=	4

▸ Children repeat the activity but start by arranging their cards as a division statement, as $\square \div 4 = 5$, for example.

▸ Write a multiplication sentence on the board or on a large sheet of paper, for example $7 \times 4 = 28$. *What else do we know? What other sentences can we write? Who can write another multiplication sentence? Who can write a division sentence?* Write $4 \times 7 = 28$, $28 \div 4 = 7$ and $28 \div 7 = 4$ on the board. Repeat, starting with a division sentence, for example $18 \div 6 = 3$.

Feedback

Can each child:

▸ say or write a division statement corresponding to a multiplication statement?

▸ say or write a multiplication statement corresponding to a division statement?

Does anyone need to use apparatus to work out the answer to a division calculation?

Is anyone confused by the order of numbers in the calculation, writing, for example, '$4 \div 28 = 7$'?

Mental calculation strategies ($\times$ and $\div$)

Objective

Use doubling and halving of two-digit numbers, for example $\times 4 =$ double, double; $\times 5 = \times 10$, halve; $\times 20 = \times 10$, double; $\times 8 = \times 4$, double; $\frac{1}{4} =$ half of one-half.

Resources

- paper squares

What children are learning

- doubling is the same as multiplying by 2
- halving is the same as dividing by 2
- to partition numbers into tens and units to help with doubling and halving

Words you can use

double, twice, lots of, multiply, halve, divide

Things to note

- The strategy being taught in this lesson requires children to know doubles of numbers to 10 and doubles of multiples of 10 to 100; this knowledge is used to work out further number facts. Children will be able to make use of this particular strategy only if they are familiar with these doubles of numbers. A list could be provided to help those who have difficulty remembering number facts.
- Encourage children to realize that doubling is the opposite of halving and that if a double is known then a corresponding half is also known, for example double 4 is 8, so half of 8 is 4.
- Doubling and halving strategies could be explored over two lessons if more appropriate. Make sure that children can work confidently with one strategy before moving on to the next.

Activities

❶ **Revise doubling and halving, starting from known facts.**

- Set some doubles questions, using a variety of language such as 'plus', 'two times', 'twice', 'double', 'two lots of'. Write 34×2 on the board. *How would you solve this?* Discuss different methods, but explain that doubling 34 is a good strategy. *Does anyone know the answer to double 34? If we don't know the answer we can split the number into tens and units.*

Demonstrate partitioning numbers into tens and units and then recombining: partition 34 into 30 and 4; double each part separately, and then recombine, as shown. Ask the children to double other numbers in this way, for example 12, 25, 16, 38, 41 etc. Congratulate any children who can say the answer without showing this working out. Provide larger numbers for them to double.

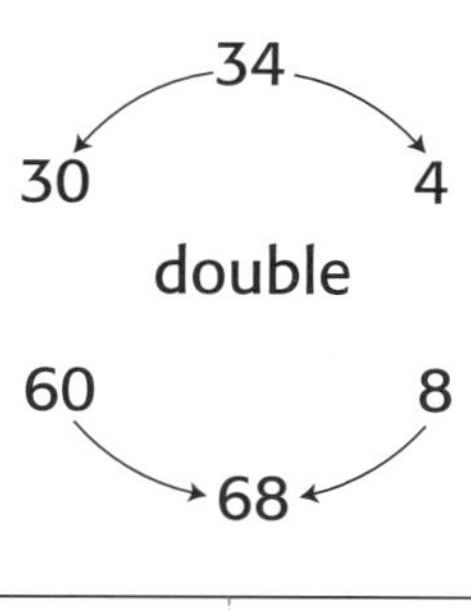

- ▶ Extend this strategy to multiplying by four. Fold a square of paper into quarters and write the same number in each section. *I want to work out thirty-two times four.* Fold the square to show just the top two sections. *What is thirty-two multiplied by two? How did you know? If the top half is worth sixty-four, what will the whole sheet be worth? Why?* Show by folding. *To multiply a number by four, we double it, and then double it again.* Show how to partition a number to work out the doubles. Provide children with numbers up to 30 or 40 to multiply by four in this way.

- ▶ Children can halve even numbers by reversing the process. Provide a list of even numbers up to about 100 for children to halve. Discuss that this is the same as dividing by two.

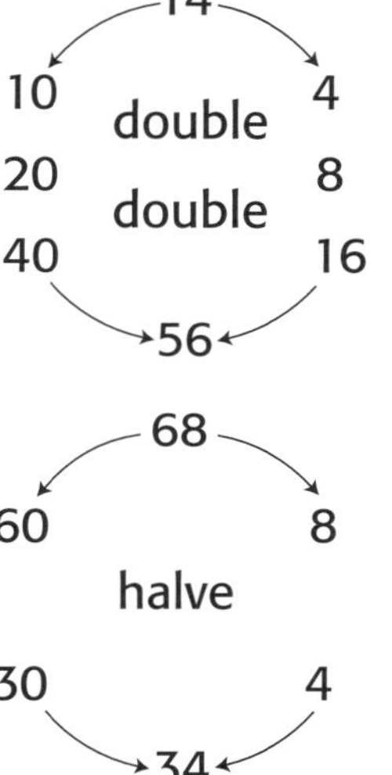

- ▶ If children are successful they can divide multiples of 4 by four, for example dividing 24, 32, 36, 48, 56, 64 by 4 by halving the number and halving it again.

- ▶ *Variations:* if appropriate, children can be introduced to other strategies, for example:
  - to multiply by 8 we double three times
  - to multiply by 5 we first multiply by 10 and then halve the answer
  - to multiply by 20 we first multiply by 10 and then double the answer.

Feedback

Can each child:
- ▶ use doubling, starting from known facts?
- ▶ use halving, starting from known facts?

Does anyone have difficulty doubling numbers in which the units digit is 5 or more?

Pencil and paper procedures (× and ÷)

Objective

Approximating first, use informal pencil and paper methods to multiply.

Resources

▸ none needed

What children are learning

a pencil and paper method of multiplication which uses place value and allows children to see clearly how multiplication works

Words you can use

times, multiply, multiplied by, partition, total, product

Things to note

▸ Children need to be able to partition or split numbers into tens and units to use this method.
▸ This method is easier for children if they realize the link between multiplying by a single-digit number and multiplying by its two-digit multiple of 10, for example $6 \times 3 = 18$, $6 \times 30 = 180$.
▸ Approaching multiplication in this way allows children to see clearly that we can split numbers into parts and multiply each separately. By splitting numbers into tens and units we are emphasizing place value.
▸ The idea that the position of a digit in a number determines its worth is known as 'place value'. Place value in our number system allows us to create an infinite series of numbers using just ten digits (0, 1, 2, 3, 4, 5, 6, 7, 8 and 9). Place-value cards can help children to appreciate that the 1 in the number 17 is worth 10 etc.

Activities

❶ **Approximate first, then use informal pencil and paper methods to multiply.**
   ▸ Write some two-digit numbers on the board, for example 34, 72, 59, and ask children to split, or partition, the numbers into tens and units, for example 30 + 4, 70 + 2 and 50 + 9, respectively. Ensure children can do this before moving on.

- Write a multiplication question on the board, for example 5 × 23. Ask children to give an approximate answer. *Roughly what is the answer going to be? What would the answer be if it was just five times twenty?* (Remind children that this can be calculated by multiplying five by two, and then by ten.) *So the answer to five times twenty-three will be a bit more than a hundred. Who can split twenty-three into tens and units?* Invite a child to write 20 + 3 on the board. Demonstrate how we use partitioning to work out 23 × 5 using the grid method. *What is five times twenty? What is five multiplied by three?* Write the answers in the boxes. *What do we do next?* Children add the two numbers and write the answer alongside. Point out that we split up the number at the beginning and now we are putting it back together. Compare the answer with the approximation. *Was our rough answer about right?*

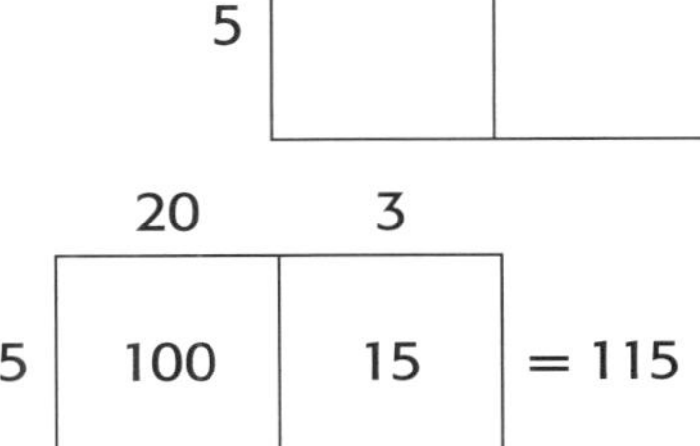

- Write further multiplication questions on the board for children to solve, for example 26 × 4, 19 × 5, 32 × 6. Easier calculations can be provided if necessary, for example 16 × 3, 14 × 5, 23 × 3. Encourage children to approximate first to get a rough idea of the expected answer.

- It may help children if questions are set in a context. For example, *I buy twenty-three packets of stickers. Each packet contains five stickers. It is hard to work out straight away how many stickers I have, but I can get a rough idea first. I can easily work out how many in twenty packets because I know that 5 × 20 = 100. I can work out how many are in the other three packets 5 × 3 = 15. So altogether in twenty-three packets I have 100 + 15 = 115.*

Feedback

Can each child:

- approximate?
- use informal pencil and paper methods to multiply?
- multiply a small number by a two-digit multiple of 10 (e.g. 5 × 30) in their head?

Who could confidently set out a multiplication using the grid method?

Objectives

Choose appropriate number operations and calculation methods to solve money and 'real-life' word problems with one or more steps.
Explain and record methods.

Resources

- coins and notes
- variety of items and price labels varying from 10p to £5

What children are learning

- to solve problems involving money
- to explain how they worked out a problem involving one or more steps

Words you can use

sort, set, coins, 1p, 2p, 5p, 10p, 20p, 50p, £1, £2, £5 note, £10 note, coin, pound, pence, penny, how many?, total, cost, pay, price, count, number, more, fewer, altogether, left, subtract, change

Things to note

- The key to this lesson is to ask a variety of questions. Children need experience of a range of vocabulary and ways of asking the same question, to ensure that they become familiar with the way in which worded questions are presented.
- Children may require plenty of practice before they can confidently write prices that involve a place-holding zero using the £·p notation, for example four pounds and two pence as £4·02 not £4·2.
- Never use a pound sign and a pence sign together when recording an amount (£3·45p).
- Children do not always notice different units. Encourage them to convert pounds to pence or vice versa to make a calculation easier, for example £1·30 − 68p = 130p − 68p = 62p.

Activities

❶ Choose appropriate number operations and calculation methods to solve money and 'real-life' word problems with one or more steps. Explain and record methods.

- Show the children a variety of items with price labels varying from 10p to £5.

Discuss the labels and ask children a range of questions relating to the prices such as:

- *How much would the jumper and the T-shirt cost altogether?*
- *What is the total cost of these two items?* (addition)
- *How much more expensive is the calculator than the jumper?*
- *How much cheaper is the ruler than the pencil case?*
- *What is the difference between these two prices?* (subtraction)
- *How much would five calculators cost?* (multiplication)
- *How many 10p stamps could I buy for £1·20?* (division)

▸ For each question, ask a child to explain how they would solve it, for example 'I think you add the two numbers', and ask all the children to write this down as a number sentence and answer it, for example 25p + £1·20 = £1·45. Encourage them to explain how they found the answer, for example 'I counted on twenty from one pound twenty pence and added five'.

▸ Ask children to draw a table of four columns with the following headings:

Item 1   Item 2   Total cost   Difference between prices

▸ Explain to the children that they should choose two items and write the prices into the first two columns, for example 80p, £1·25. They should write the total of the two prices in the third column and the difference between them in the fourth. Encourage them to choose a range of differently priced items. Continue to ask questions about their work, using a range of vocabulary, for example *How much more expensive was the pencil case than the stamp? What is the cost of the jumper plus the pencil case?* Ask more challenging questions that require them to work out an extra step, for example *How much change from £10 would you get if you bought these two items? What if a shop offered a half-price sale? How much would this cost?*

Feedback

Can each child:

▸ solve problems involving money?
▸ explain how they worked out a problem involving one or more steps?

Does anyone get confused when asked to add two prices where one is given in pounds and the other in pence, for example £1·20 + 85p?

Does anyone have difficulty identifying the operation from the context of the problem?

18 Fractions and decimals

Objectives

Use fraction notation.
Recognize fractions that are several parts of a whole and find fractions of shapes.

Resources

▸ rectangles of paper (and possibly circles)
▸ interlocking cubes

What children are learning

▸ that fractions are equal parts of things
▸ that numbers can be split into fractional parts
▸ that fractions can be several parts of a whole

Words you can use

fraction, half, third, quarter, fifth, tenth, mixed number

Things to note

▸ When children first encounter fractions in school, it is usually in relation to areas of shapes, for example half of a circle, one-quarter of a square etc. Children often build up a visual picture of these fractions without realizing the significance of the notation, for example that $\frac{1}{2}$ means one out of two equal parts.
▸ As children's understanding of fractions grows, they will begin to realize that any number, shape or set of objects can be split into *equal* parts to make fractions. For example, twenty can be split into four equal parts to make quarters; each of the quarters is worth five.
▸ Children need to become confident using the language of fractions. Encourage them to read the fractions aloud, for example $\frac{3}{5}$ as 'three-fifths'.

Activities

❶ Recognize fractions that are several parts of a whole.

▸ Give each child a rectangle and ask them to fold it into smaller pieces of the same size. Ask children to show everyone else their rectangle. (If they find this difficult, show them how to fold a rectangle into halves, quarters, eighths etc.)

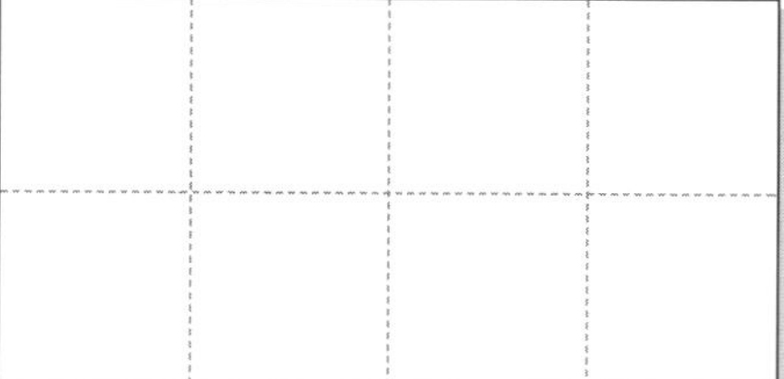

Look at each rectangle in turn. *How many equal pieces are there? What fraction is each piece? How many eighths make the whole rectangle? Let's count: one eighth, two eighths, three eighths … eight eighths.*

▸ Ask a child to colour in some pieces while the rest count. *Sam has coloured three eighths red.*

▸ Ask children to colour in various segments of their rectangle, using different colours if they wish. They can then stick the rectangle onto paper and below it write what they have done.

Variation: children can be given paper circles to explore halves, quarters and eighths in the same way. (They may need help folding the circles into eighths.)

▸ Ask children to stick cubes together to make a 4×2 block in a variety of colours. Ask questions about the blocks. *How many cubes are in your block? What fraction of the block is one cube? How do we write one-eighth? What fraction of the block is red?* etc.

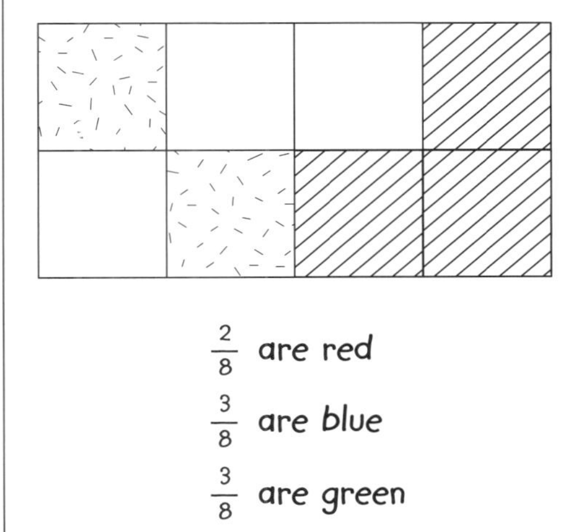

$\frac{2}{8}$ are red

$\frac{3}{8}$ are blue

$\frac{3}{8}$ are green

▸ Ask the children to draw a 4×2 grid on squared paper. *What fraction of the grid is one square? Colour one-eighth of the grid red. Colour five-eighths of the grid blue. How much is left?* Ask children to choose how to colour the squares in a second 4×2 grid. Discuss the fractions they have created and ask them to record these as they did for the paper shapes.

Variation: children can explore sixths using a 3×2 array of blocks.

Feedback

Can each child:

▸ recognize fractions that are several parts of a whole?
▸ find fractions of shapes?
▸ identify what sort of fraction a shape is divided into?
▸ count in fractions while pointing to each part?

Does anyone know how many of a fraction make one whole?

Fractions and decimals

Objectives

Use fraction notation.
Recognize fractions that are mixed numbers.

Resources

- circles of paper cut into quarters
- Blu-tack
- large sheets of paper

What children are learning

- that fractions are equal parts of things
- that numbers can be split into fractional parts
- that fractions can be several parts of a whole
- that numbers that consist of both a whole number and a fraction, for example $3\frac{1}{2}$, $3\frac{2}{5}$, $4\frac{1}{4}$, are called mixed numbers

Words you can use

fraction, half, third, quarter, fifth, tenth

Things to note

- When children first encounter fractions in school, it is usually in relation to areas of shapes, for example half of a circle, one-quarter of a square etc. Children often build up a visual picture of these fractions without realizing the significance of the notation, for example that $\frac{1}{2}$ means one out of two equal parts.
- As children's understanding of fractions grows, they will begin to realize that any number, shape or set of objects can be split into *equal* parts to make fractions. For example, twenty can be split into four equal parts to make quarters; each of the quarters is worth five.
- Numbers that consist of both a whole number and a fraction, for example $1\frac{1}{2}$, $3\frac{2}{5}$, $4\frac{1}{4}$, are called mixed numbers. You may need to remind children of this.
- Children are often unsure of how to read and write mixed numbers. They will need plenty of practice in this.

Activities

❶ Recognize mixed numbers.

▸ Cut several paper circles into quarters. Hold up one quarter. *What fraction of a circle is this?* Blu-tack four quarters on the board, one by one, to form a circle, asking the children to count with you as you do so: *one quarter, two quarters, three quarters, four quarters.* You could ask a child to write the fractions on the board as you count, recording $\frac{1}{4}, \frac{2}{4}, \frac{3}{4}, \frac{4}{4}$. (They may need help with this.) *What have we made? One whole. So four quarters make one whole, or one.*

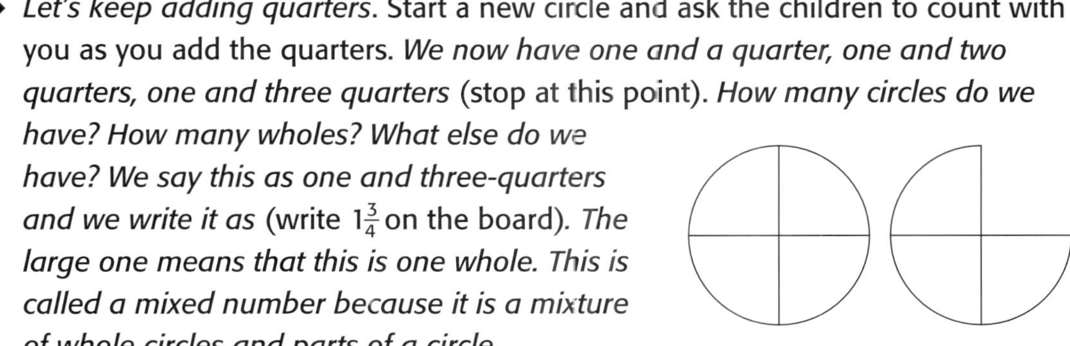

▸ *Let's keep adding quarters.* Start a new circle and ask the children to count with you as you add the quarters. *We now have one and a quarter, one and two quarters, one and three quarters* (stop at this point). *How many circles do we have? How many wholes? What else do we have? We say this as one and three-quarters and we write it as* (write $1\frac{3}{4}$ on the board). *The large one means that this is one whole. This is called a mixed number because it is a mixture of whole circles and parts of a circle.*

▸ Continue adding quarters until you reach $2\frac{1}{4}$. *How many circles are there now? How could we write that?*

▸ Give children some paper quarter circles, a large sheet of paper and some Blu-tack. Ask them to see how many circles they can make using all the quarters and to record this in figures and in words.

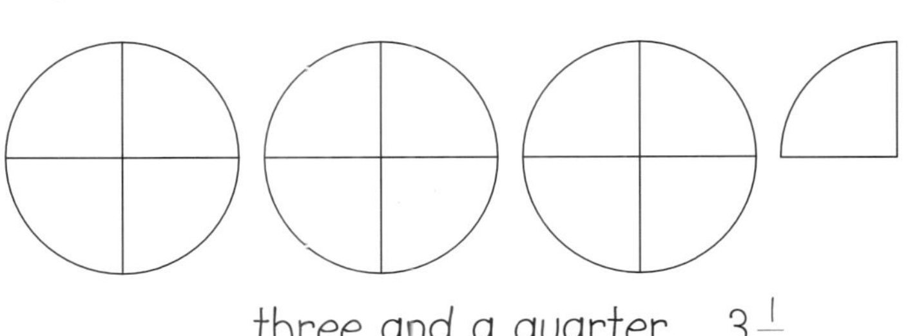

▸ This could be repeated with other fractions.

Feedback

Can each child:

▸ use fraction notation?

▸ recognize mixed numbers?

▸ read a mixed number, for example $2\frac{1}{4}$ as 'two and a quarter'?

Given a picture of a mixed number (for example, $1\frac{3}{4}$ circles shown above), which children can describe this using a mixed number?

Objective

Find simple fractions of quantities.

Resources

- metre stick
- pipe-cleaners
- 20 cm strips of paper marked in cm

What children are learning

- that fractions are equal parts of things
- that numbers and quantities can be split into fractional parts
- that finding one-half is the same as dividing by two, finding one-third is the same as dividing by three etc.
- to use division to find fractions of amounts

Words you can use

fraction, half, third, quarter, fifth, tenth, divide

Things to note

- Encourage children to read fractions aloud, for example $\frac{7}{8}$ should be read as 'seven-eighths'.
- Many children struggle with the way in which fractions are written: $\frac{3}{4}, \frac{7}{8}, \frac{5}{12}$ etc. The idea that a number less than one is written using two numbers, each of which is more than one, can be confusing. In order to use this notation with confidence, children have to understand the role of each number, so $\frac{3}{4}$ means three out of four, and $\frac{7}{8}$ means seven out of eight.

Activities

❶ **Find simple fractions of quantities.**

- Show children a metre stick, clearly marked in centimetres. *How many centimetres long is this stick? How many centimetres long is half of this stick? Who can place this pipe-cleaner to split the stick in half? So half of one hundred centimetres is fifty centimetres.* Record this on the board.
- *Who can place pipe-cleaners to split the stick into quarters? How many equal pieces must there be to make quarters? So how many centimetres long is a quarter of the stick?* Record this on the board as '$\frac{1}{4}$ of 100 cm is 25 cm'.

- Remove the pipe-cleaners. *Can anyone divide the stick into tenths? How many equal pieces must there be if the sections are tenths?* Help a child to do this, or show them yourself if children are unsure. *How many centimetres long is one-tenth of the stick?* Record this on the board as '$\frac{1}{10}$ of 100 cm is 10 cm'.
- Give each pair of children three 20-cm strips of paper, marked in centimetres.

Explain that you want them to draw lines to divide one strip into halves, one into quarters, and one into tenths. They need to discuss how to do this and then record the following: '$\frac{1}{2}$ of 20 cm is …', '$\frac{1}{4}$ of 20 cm is …', '$\frac{1}{10}$ of 20 cm is …'.
- Some children may be able to go on to find one-fifth, or to work with different-length strips.

Feedback

Can each child find simple fractions of quantities?

Do any children have problems finding any fraction other than $\frac{1}{2}$ or $\frac{1}{4}$?

Which children are confident that to find one-tenth of the strip you need to divide it into ten equal pieces? (Children often try to divide it into sections of ten squares instead.)

Did anyone work out $20 \div 10$ to find where to draw the lines to split the strip into tenths?

Understanding addition and subtraction/ Mental calculation strategies (+ and –)

Objectives

Consolidate understanding of subtraction as the inverse of addition.
Find a small difference by counting up.
Use the relationship between + and –.

Resources

▸ none needed

What children are learning

▸ that addition is the opposite, or inverse, of subtraction, and vice versa
▸ to use addition to check subtraction calculations, and vice versa
▸ to realize that it can be easier to turn subtraction questions into addition questions and then count up from the smaller number, for example 403 – 396 can be thought of as 'what's the difference between 396 and 403?', and can be solved by counting up from 396 to 403, which is 7

Words you can use

difference, addition, subtraction, counting up, counting on, tens, hundreds, add, plus, and, makes, equals, minus, subtract, take away, difference

Things to note

▸ Children should realize that addition is the opposite, or inverse, of subtraction, and vice versa. This means we can 'undo' addition with subtraction, and vice versa, so 15 + 4 = 19 and 19 – 4 = 15 etc.
▸ It is also important that children realize that if we know one number sentence we can work out three more by rearranging the numbers, for example if we know 18 + 12 = 30 we can create the addition sentence 12 + 18 = 30 and the subtraction sentences 30 – 12 = 18 and 30 – 18 = 12.
▸ Encouraging children to count on along a number line can give them confidence when crossing a hundreds boundary, for example 98 to 101 or 297 to 306. Alternatively they can do this as a check.
▸ Where possible, encourage children *not* to count on in ones, but to use number bonds and place value to count on in known jumps. Blank number lines can be helpful.

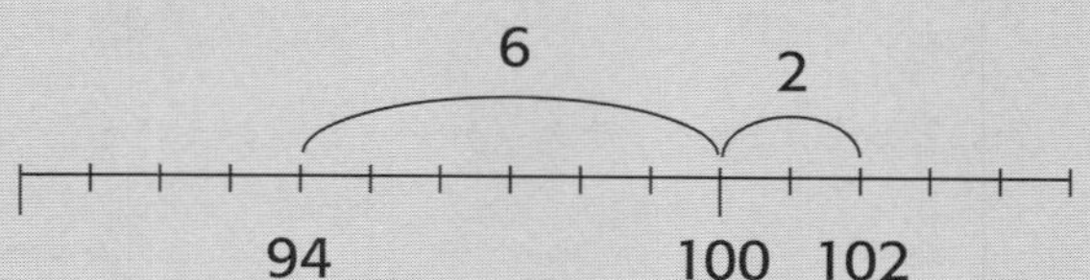

Activities

❶ Explore subtraction as the inverse of addition. Practise counting up.

▸ Write an addition sentence on the board or on a large sheet of paper, for example
96 + 5 = 101. *What else do we know? What other sentences can we write? Who
can write another addition sentence?* (5 + 96 = 101) *Who can write a subtraction
sentence? And another one?* Write 101 − 96 = 5 and 101 − 5 = 96. Repeat,
starting with a subtraction question, for example 104 − 95 = . *What is the
difference between these two numbers?* Discuss that 100 comes between the
two numbers and ask children to use this to find the answer. Show how they can
do this by counting up from the smaller number, using a number line:

Ask children to write the
related subtraction sentence
(104 − 9 = 95) and the two
related addition sentences,

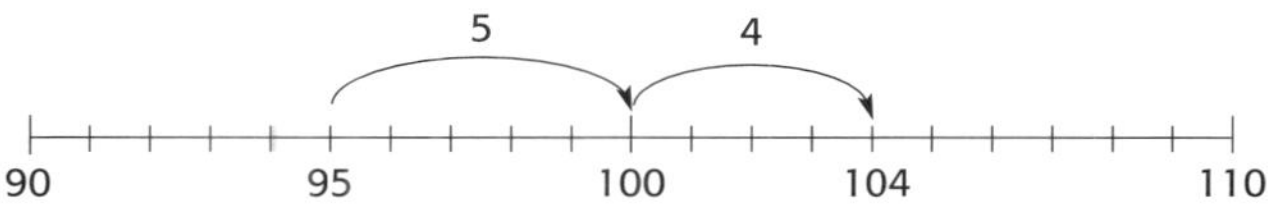

9 + 95 = 104 and 95 + 9 = 104. Repeat for further difference questions that
cross either a tens or a hundreds boundary, for example 95 − 87, 106 − 98, until
the children are confident about finding the difference and generating the three
related statements.

▸ Write 405 − 394 on the board. *What hundreds number comes between these two
numbers?* Ask children to find the difference between these numbers. Show how
they can do this by counting
up from the smaller number.
When children are confident
about crossing a hundreds

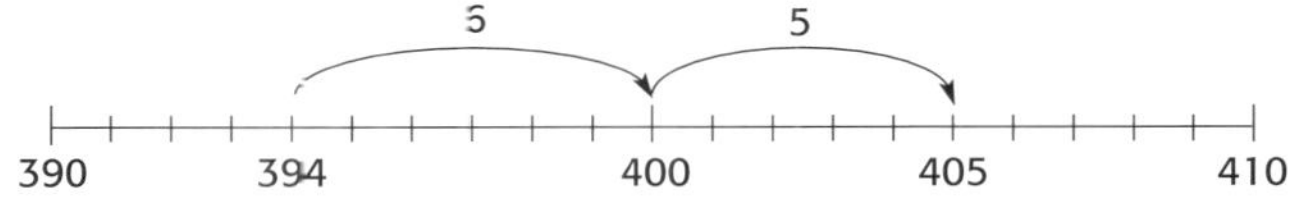

boundary in this way, write pairs of three-digit numbers on the board that are less
than ten apart but are separated by a hundreds boundary, for example 198 and
203, 294 and 302, 396 and 403 etc. Ask children to find the difference in the
same way.

▸ *Variation:* children can explore numbers either side of a thousands boundary, for
example 1005 − 997.

Feedback

Can each child:
▸ find small differences by counting up?
▸ identify the multiple of 100 between numbers?

Is anyone still reliant on counting on in ones?

Does everyone understand subtraction as the inverse of addition?

Objective

Develop written methods for addition of whole numbers less than 1000.

Resources

▸ none needed

What children are learning

▸ a written method for adding numbers that are too large to add mentally
▸ to approximate before calculating

Words you can use

sum, total, number, order, addition, check, add

Things to note

▸ Children will naturally approximate before calculating to give themselves an idea of whether the numbers they are considering are suitable.
▸ Children should be able to add any two-digit numbers mentally before being introduced to standard written methods for addition.
▸ These activities allow children to work in whichever way is appropriate for them. This may involve working mentally and jotting things down informally, for example:

$23 + 57$

or using a more formal method, for example:

$$\begin{array}{r} 23 \\ +\,57 \\ \hline 70 \\ 10 \\ \hline 80 \end{array}$$

Activities

❶ Develop written methods for addition of whole numbers less than 1000.

  ▸ Write about twelve single- and two-digit numbers on the board, for example 23, 8, 78, 91, 6, 57, 38, 45, 11, 66, 7, 84. Ask the children to work in pairs or in groups of three. They will have three or four minutes to add whichever pairs of numbers they choose, trying to get as close to a target number as possible. *I'm going to set you a target number. Add two of these numbers to get as close to the target as you can. The first target number is 120.*

The group (or pair) compare answers and the child whose answer was nearest to the target wins a counter. A second counter can be awarded if the target is hit exactly. Alternatively the winner can announce the target for the next round. Further targets can include 135, 150, 162, 180 etc.

84	57	91
+ 38	+ 66	+ 23
12	13	4
110	110	110
122	123	114

  ▸ Children can be set different tasks, including winning a counter for:
  - reaching a total between 170 and 180 or between 200 and 210
  - finding which two numbers give a total of 114 (91 + 23)
  - finding which three numbers give a total of 173 (78 + 57 + 38)
  - making a total of 95 in two different ways, for example 57 + 38 and 84 + 11.

  ▸ *Variation:* three-digit numbers can be introduced if appropriate. Write 39, 42, 319, 6, 204, 64, 27, 80, 172, 9 on the board. Targets might include finding numbers with a total as close as possible to 250, 400, 500 etc., a number between 300 and 320, between 350 and 360 etc.

Feedback

Can each child:
  ▸ add two whole numbers less than 100 using a written method?
  ▸ add two whole numbers less than 1000 using a written method?

If children are using a formal written method, can they explain each step as they work through the calculation?

Did any children add pairs of numbers randomly, without using estimates to help them get close to the target?

Rapid recall of number facts (× and ÷)

Objective

Derive doubles of multiples of 10 to 500 and corresponding halves.

Resources

- **PCM 5**, one copy for each pair
- counters in two colours
- number cards of the multiples of 10 from 10 to 500 (10, 20, 30 … 500)

What children are learning

- to understand the words double and half
- to know or find quickly the doubles of multiples of 10 to 500, for example double 60, double 150, double 400
- to know or find quickly the corresponding halves, for example half of 120, half of 300, half of 800

Words you can use

double, twice, half, number, multiply, divide

Things to note

- To use the strategy taught in this lesson, children need to be aware of the link between doubling single-digit numbers and doubling related two- and three-digit numbers, for example:

$$3 + 3 = 6$$
$$30 + 30 = 60$$
$$300 + 300 = 600$$

- When playing the game, a list of the doubles to 20 could be provided for children who have difficulty remembering the facts.
- Encourage children to realize that doubling is the opposite of halving and that if a double is known, a corresponding half is also known, for example double 150 is 300, so half of 300 is 150.
- You may wish to spend more than one lesson on these activities.

Activities

❶ **Double numbers to 100.**
   Ask children to say pairs of doubles, beginning with a single-digit number and followed by the related multiple of 10, for example 'double 8 is 16 and double 80 is 160'.

❷ Double numbers to 500.

Give each pair of children a copy of **PCM 5**, counters in two colours and a set of number cards or slips of paper showing multiples of 10 from 10 to 500. Place the cards face down in a pile. Children take turns to turn over a card, to double the number and to put a counter in their colour on that number on the grid on the PCM. The winner is the first player to get four counters in a line in any direction. Three in a line can be used for a quicker game. A calculator can be used to check answers if necessary, but encourage children to use their knowledge that if double 8 is 16, then double 80 is 160.

260	180	720	980	420
480	680	840	400	160
700	300	100	620	240
460	380	860	40	320
600	1000	740	880	560
960	140	20	640	900
340	220	760	360	540
80	820	500	280	440
800	780	920	120	60
580	940	200	520	660

❸ Halve numbers to 200.

Write the multiples of 20 from 20 to 200 (20, 40, 60 … 200) in random order on a large sheet of paper. *These are the answers to some of the doubles questions you have been doing. What doubles question is 160 the answer to?* Write 'double 80 = 160' on the board or on the sheet of paper. *We can also describe this in another way.* Write 'half of 160 = 80' and ask children to read it aloud. Point to other numbers on the sheet and ask *What is half of …?* Record the halves of all the numbers in this way, encouraging children to use their knowledge that half of 16 is 8, so half of 160 is 80.

❹ Halve numbers to 1000.

This game can be played by groups of 2–5 players. Children cover the numbers on the grid on **PCM 5** with cubes. They take turns to remove a cube and halve the number revealed. If they are correct they keep the cube, if not the cube is replaced. The winner is the player who finishes with most cubes.

Feedback

Can each child:
▸ derive doubles of multiples of 10 to 500?
▸ derive corresponding halves?

Does any child find it difficult to double multiples of 10 in which the tens digit is 5 or more, for example 270?

Can children explain their methods?

Place value, ordering, rounding

Objective
Multiply and divide an integer up to 1000 by 10; understand the effect.

Resources
- calculators
- 10–100 number cards
- cards showing three-digit numbers

What children are learning
- that to multiply a number by 10 we move the digits one place to the left and fill the space with a zero, for example:
- that to divide a number by 10 we move the digits one place to the right, for example:

H	T	U	
	5	2	× 10
5	2	0	

H	T	U	
5	2	0	÷ 10
	5	2	

Words you can use
multiply, divide, ten, hundred, digit, place value

Things to note
- Avoid telling children to 'add a zero' when multiplying by 10. This phrase can be confusing because we are not actually *adding* anything. We are multiplying. When we *add* zero to a number the number stays the same, for example $6 + 0 = 6$. Also, this phrase works for whole numbers only and causes confusion when children meet decimals, for example $5.4 \times 10 = 54$, not 5.40.
- Focus attention on the movement of the digits one place to the left when we multiply by 10 and two places to the left when we multiply by 100. Children benefit from practical experience of physically 'moving' digits, for example using number cards on a place-value board.

Activities
❶ Multiply an integer up to 1000 by 10; understand the effect.
- Give each child a calculator. Ask them to key in a two-digit number, for example 25. *What will happen to this number if we multiply it by ten?* Ask the children to write their prediction on paper, for example $25 \times 10 = 250$. Now ask them to enter ⊗ ① ⓪ ⊜. *Is the answer the same as you thought?* Children should tick or cross their prediction, writing the correct answer if necessary. Discuss any wrong answers. *Why did you think the answer would be that?*

- Ask the children to choose cards from a set of 10–100 number cards. They write their prediction each time and then multiply the number by 10 on the calculator to check. Draw their attention to the movement of each of the digits one place to the left. *What is happening each time?* This can be clearly seen by entering the chosen numbers and the answers when multiplied by 10 into a table, as shown. Alternatively, demonstrate using number cards on a place-value board.

H	T	U
	3	7
3	7	0
	6	4
6	4	0

- Give children some cards on which you have written three-digit numbers for children to multiply by 10. Children predict and check as before.

❷ Divide an integer up to 1000 by 10; understand the effect.

- Ask children to key into the calculator a two-digit multiple of 10, for example 70. *What will happen to this number if we divide it by ten?* Ask the children to write down their prediction on paper, for example 70 ÷ 10 = 7. Now ask them to enter ÷ ① ⓪ ⩵. *Is the answer the same as you thought?* Children should tick or cross their prediction, as above, writing in the correct answer if necessary. Children can also practise dividing by 10 using number cards and a place-value board to show how the digits move one place to the right.
- Give the children cards on which you have written three-digit multiples of 10, for example 350, 790. Children predict and check the effect of dividing these numbers, as before.
- Shuffle a set of about twenty 0–100 number cards with cards showing three-digit multiples of 10. Turn over a card, for example 350. On the board write □ × 10 = 350. *What number do we multiply by ten to make 350?* (35). For a two-digit number write this on the board as, for example, □ ÷ 10 = 63. *What number do you divide by ten to make sixty-three?* (630)
- Check the children's answers. Each child can be given a counter for a correct answer.

Feedback

Can each child:

- multiply by 10 and explain what is happening?
- divide by 10 and explain what is happening?

Is anyone confused about which way to move the digits?

Who can explain why 36 ÷ 10 = 360 must be wrong? (Dividing a whole number by 10 will give you a smaller answer.)

Place value, ordering, rounding

Objectives

Read and write the vocabulary of comparing and ordering numbers.
Use symbols =, <, > correctly.
Give a number lying between two others.

Resources

- about twenty cards, each showing a four-digit number
- sign cards (< and >)

What children are learning

- to put four-digit numbers in order
- to read and write the vocabulary of comparing and ordering numbers, for example 'first', 'second', 'last', 'between', 'next to', 'larger than' etc.
- to use the symbols < and > to mean 'less than' and 'more than', respectively
- to give a number that lies between two others

Words you can use

first, second, third etc., next to, between, last, larger/smaller than

Things to note

- The idea that the position of a digit in a number determines its worth is known as 'place value'. Place value in our number system allows us to create an infinite series of numbers using just ten digits (0, 1, 2, 3, 4, 5, 6, 7, 8 and 9).
- Children need to be confident in ordering two-digit and three-digit numbers before they are able to tackle four-digit numbers. If children struggle with the activities below, do each of them with two-digit numbers using 0–99 number cards and three-digit numbers using 0–999 number cards before extending to four digits.
- Children need to be able to read 243 < 612 as 'two hundred and forty-three is less than six hundred and twelve' and 612 > 243 as 'six hundred and twelve is greater than two hundred and forty-three'.

Activities

❶ **Compare and order numbers.**
You will need about twenty four-digit number cards for each group of three children. Place the cards face down in a pile. Children each turn over a card, and the child whose number lies between the other two numbers, in this case 4627, wins a counter.

| 1358 | 4627 | 6813 |

Continue until all the cards have been used. If children find this difficult, encourage them to compare the numbers by looking first at the thousands (left-hand) digits. Only if these are the same do they need to look at the hundreds digits. Ask them to explain what is happening, for example 'David picked 3458 and Hannah had 8513. I had 6267 and that's in between'. Each of the numbers should be said in full as 'three thousand four hundred and fifty-eight' rather than 'three four five eight'.

❷ **Use symbols =, < and >.**
Children work in pairs. Shuffle the number cards again, divide them into two piles and place each face down on the table. They each turn over a card; the child whose card has the higher number has the chance to win a counter. To do so, they must arrange the two cards with a card correctly showing either < or > between them. If children find this difficult, show how the symbols can be thought of as a pair of jaws which is always about to eat the larger number.

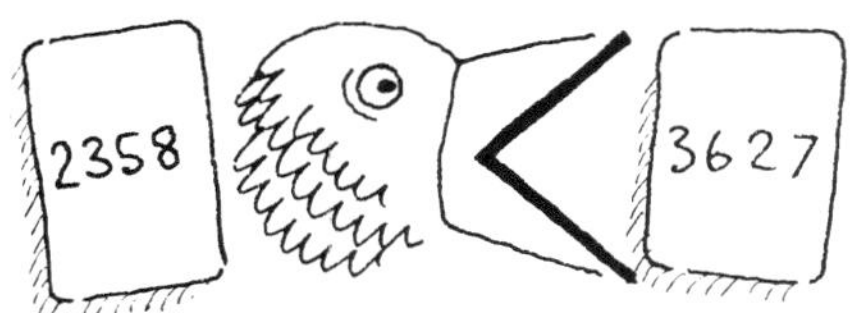

❸ **Give a number that lies between two others.**
Repeat activity 2 with the < and > cards but this time to win a counter the children must also say a number that lies between the two numbers on the cards. Ask them to explain each time, for example 'two thousand three hundred and forty-one is more than one thousand seven hundred and ninety-six, and two thousand is between them'. Continue until all the cards have been used.

Feedback

Can each child:
- ▸ read and write the vocabulary of comparing and ordering numbers?
- ▸ use the symbols < and > to mean 'less than' and 'more than', respectively?
- ▸ give a number that lies between two others?

Does anyone get confused about which symbol, < or >, to use in a statement?

Which children could explain how they knew that 4213 is smaller than 6005?

Objective
Round any positive number less than 1000 to the nearest 10.

Resources
- 0–9 number cards
- cards showing multiples of 10 from 100
- washing line and pegs
- cards, each showing a three-digit number between 100 and 200

What children are learning
to round any three-digit number to the nearest 10

Words you can use
round, nearest, numbers, ten, multiple

Things to note
- When rounding numbers like 5, 15, 25 … the convention is to round up to the nearest ten, rather than down. Discuss with children that numbers like these are exactly between multiples of 10. This can easily be demonstrated on a number line.
- When rounding, children often make the mistake of looking only at the left-hand digit, so they would round 135, 136, 137, 138, and 139 to 130 rather than to 140. This can be remedied by helping the child to position numbers on a number line marked from 100 to 200 in tens, and then to see the tens number that each number is nearest to.

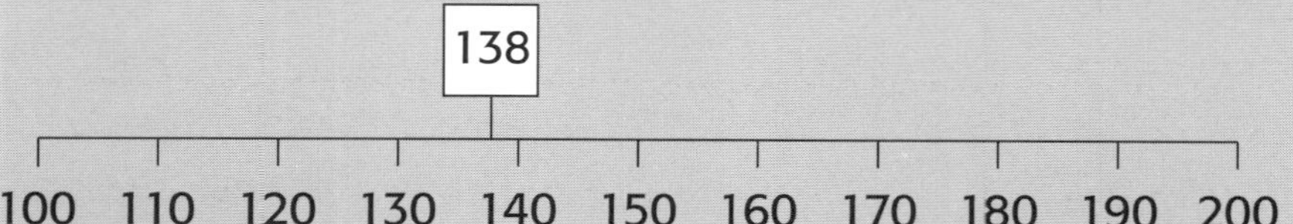

It becomes clear that 138, for example, is closer to 140 than to 130.
- This activity begins with revision of rounding two-digit numbers to the nearest ten.

Activities

1 Round numbers to 100 to the nearest 10.

Children do this activity in pairs. Each pair needs two sets of 0–9 number cards shuffled together. Ask each child to write a list of the multiples of 10 up to 100. Children take turns to take two number cards and arrange them to form a two-digit number, for example 53. The number created should be rounded to the nearest ten and written next to that multiple of 10 on the list; this multiple of 10 can then be crossed out. The winner is the first child to cross out all the numbers on their list.

10
20
30
40
50   53
60
70
80
90
100

2 Round numbers to 1000 to the nearest 10.

▸ Equally space number cards showing 100, 110, 120, 130, 140 … 200 on a washing line or piece of string.

Ask children to pick a card from a set of three-digit numbers between 100 and 200, for example 167. Explain that you want them to put their number on the line where they think it should go. *Which tens number is your number nearest to?* Remind them that this process is called *rounding*. Children continue to pick cards and peg them in the right place, each time explaining what they are doing, for example 'My number is 167. It rounds to 170'.

▸ Replace the cards on the line with cards that show 200, 210, 220 … 300, or 300, 310, 320 … 400 etc. and continue the activity.

▸ Give some practical examples, such as *There were 382 CDs in the shop. Roughly how many were there, rounded to the nearest 10?* (380) *There are about 640 conkers on the tree. How many might there be exactly?* (between 635 and 644)

Feedback

Can each child round numbers to 1000 to the nearest 10?

Which children are able to round numbers accurately where the multiple of 10 is also a multiple of 100, for example 397 → 400?

Reading numbers from scales

Objective

Recognize negative numbers in context: number line, thermometer.

Resources

▸ number line (or thermometer) marked from ⁻10 to 10
▸ counter
▸ dice

What children are learning

▸ to appreciate and recognize the numbers 'on the other side' of zero
▸ to understand that ⁻2 is less than ⁻1 even though 2 is larger than 1

Words you can use

add, plus, and, sum, total, makes, equals, minus, subtract, take away, negative, minus, zero, temperature, degrees

Things to note

▸ Counting forwards and backwards in different sized steps helps children to gain an understanding of how numbers relate to each other, including negative numbers. Children build up a picture in their minds of where numbers are, and over time are able to visualize how many more or less a number is than another without needing to count.
▸ Refer to ⁻1, ⁻2 etc. as 'minus one', 'minus two' etc. and describe these numbers collectively as 'negative numbers'.
▸ When comparing the sizes of negative numbers children often fail to understand that a number like ⁻2 is less than ⁻1.
▸ A number line provides children with a visual image to support their understanding of negative numbers.

Activities

❶ **Count back in ones including below zero.**
  ▸ Show children a number line or thermometer that includes numbers less than zero, for example from ⁻10 to 10.

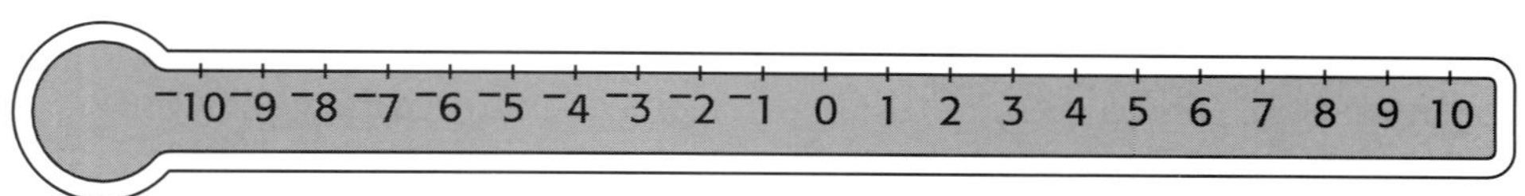

Ask children to count backwards from 10 in ones as you point to the numbers. Describe the temperature getting colder and move a counter down the number line from 10 to 0. *When the temperature is zero outside, water begins to freeze. When we are talking about temperature these numbers are called degrees.* Continue to move the counter to the left, past zero, while you count *minus one, minus two* … etc. Explain that it is getting colder and colder. Encourage children to discuss cold days and the clothes they would wear.

▸ As a whole group, play a game using the number line. Split the group into two teams. One team is 'getting colder', the other is 'getting hotter'. Place a counter on 0 to start. The teams take turns to roll a dice. The 'getting colder' team moves the counter in the negative direction, towards ⁻10. The 'getting hotter' team moves in a positive direction, towards 10. As each move is made, the children should describe what is happening to the temperature, for example 'The temperature is falling three degrees from minus one to minus four.' 'It is getting hotter by five degrees. The temperature has risen from minus four to one'. The winner is the team who reaches 10 or ⁻10 first.

▸ Give each child a calculator and ask them to key in 10 and then to repeatedly key in ⊖①⊜ (or use the constant function ⊖⊖①⊜⊜⊜ …). Each time the equals key is pressed, the display will show numbers counting down from 10 to below zero. Encourage the children to say these numbers aloud. Similarly start with ⁻10 and repeatedly key in ⊕①⊜ to generate a sequence growing in ones from ⁻10 towards 10.

▸ Discuss pairs of negative numbers and ask the children to say which is larger, for example is ⁻5 larger than ⁻2?

Feedback

Can each child:

▸ count back in ones to below zero?
▸ recognize the numbers 'on the other side' of zero?
▸ understand that ⁻2 is less than ⁻1 even though 2 is larger than 1?

Understanding addition and subtraction/ Mental calculation strategies (+ and −)

Objectives

Understand the principle (not the name) of the commutative law for +, not −.
Add several small numbers by finding pairs that total 10, or 9 or 11.

Resources

- several sets of 0–20 number cards
- 1–10 dice
- counters
- 8 × 4 grids of the numbers 9–40

What children are learning

- to appreciate that three and four numbers can be added together
- to do this using different calculation strategies, for example putting the larger number first or finding pairs of numbers that total 10

Words you can use

and, add, plus, makes, equals, altogether, same as, total

Things to note

- Children first learn to add two numbers together, which sometimes gives them a limited understanding of addition. Their experience is initially grouping two sets of objects and counting them to find the total. The fact that more than two numbers can be added can cause initial difficulty for some children. This lesson includes adding three or four numbers together.
- Use the range of vocabulary listed above so that children experience several ways of describing addition, for example 'three plus five', 'three and five', 'three add five', 'the total of three and five', 'three and five altogether' etc.
- Encourage children to use strategies other than counting on.

Activities

❶ **Add several small numbers by finding pairs that total 10, or 9 or 11.**

- Start with several sets of 0–10 number cards shuffled together. Quickly turn over four cards, allowing all children to see them at the same time. The child who finds the total first wins a counter. If one child scores two counters in a row, they can turn over the next four cards for the next question (to give the other children a chance). After each question discuss the strategy *How did you work it out so quickly?*

What did you notice? For example 'eight and two make ten, so eight plus two plus nine is nineteen; ten add nine is nineteen' or 'I know that double eight is sixteen and I subtracted one to make fifteen and then added four' etc. Emphasize that we can add numbers in any order and the answer will be the same.

▷ *Variations:* children can add three cards to begin with. Several cards from 0 to 20 can be added to increase the level of difficulty.

▸ Give each child four 1–10 dice and a grid containing the numbers 9–40. Each child rolls the dice, adds the numbers and then colours in the total on the grid. How many of the numbers can the children colour? Remind them of the strategies of putting the larger number first and finding pairs that make 10.

9	10	11	12
13	14	15	16
17	18	19	20
21	22	23	24
25	26	27	28
29	30	31	32
33	34	35	36
37	38	39	40

▷ *Variations:* children can be given larger numbers to add by rolling three 1–10 dice and choosing a 0–20 number card for the fourth number. Children can record their additions by crossing numbers from a simple list of the numbers from 4 to 50, or colouring in answers on a 100 square. Children can roll three dice rather than four, recording on a 3–30 grid.

▸ Write several questions on the board where one of the numbers to be added is missing, for example $8 + 4 + \square + 9 = 28$, $\square + 16 + 4 = 28$ etc. Work through the questions, discussing strategies for working out the missing number.

Feedback

Can each child:
▸ add three numbers, using mental calculation strategies?
▸ add four numbers, using mental calculation strategies?

Which strategies do children use with confidence?

Can children explain their strategy?

Is anyone still reliant on counting on in ones?

Objectives

Partition into tens and units, adding tens first.
Add three two-digit multiples of 10.

Resources

- copies of table shown below
- 10–100 number cards
- dartboard (or picture)
- sets of number cards of multiples of 10 (20, 30 … 90)

What children are learning

- to partition (split) a two-digit number into tens and units
- to use this skill to add three two-digit numbers
- to add three two-digit multiples of 10, for example 30 + 80 + 40

Words you can use

tens, units, ones, number, partition, add, total

Things to note

- Children need to be able to split, or partition, a number like 53 into tens and units, as in 'five tens and three units' but they also need to appreciate the size of the number as a whole. Partitioning into 50 + 3 as well as 'five tens and three units' can help.
- The idea that the position of a digit in a number determines its worth is known as 'place value'. Place value in our number system allows us to create an infinite series of numbers using just ten digits (0, 1, 2, 3, 4, 5, 6, 7, 8 and 9). Place-value cards can help children to appreciate that the 1 in the number 17 is worth ten etc.
- Emphasize the link between adding single-digit numbers and multiples of 10, for example 3 + 6 = 9 and 30 + 60 = 90.

Activities

❶ Partition into tens and units and recombine.

Children work in pairs. Give each child several copies of the table shown here. They take turns to turn over a card from a shuffled set of 10–100 cards, for example 83, partition the number into tens and units (80 + 3) and write it in the table as 83 = 80 + 3. The first player to fill the table is the winner. Children can play the game several times.

	= 10 +
	= 20 +
	= 30 +
	= 40 +
	= 50 +
	= 60 +
	= 70 +
83	= 80 + 3
	= 90 +

❷ Add three two-digit numbers by partitioning into tens and units and recombining.

Point to a two-digit number on the dartboard, for example 13. Explain that this is where your dart has hit. Ask children to write down the number. Repeat for two more numbers, for example 11 and 15. Ask children to add the numbers by splitting them into tens and units and then recombining to find a total, adding the tens first, for example $(10 + 3) + (10 + 1) + (10 + 5) = 39$. Initially avoid the units adding to ten or more. Once children are confident with partitioning and recombining, move on to include numbers where the units add to more than ten, for example $14 + 18 + 13 = (10 + 4) + (10 + 8) + (10 + 3) = 30 + 15 = 45$. If children are confident, introduce larger numbers by 'hitting' doubles on the board: *This dart has landed on double eighteen. What number is that?*

❸ Add three two-digit multiples of 10.

- Draw a dartboard with nine sections. Ask a child to point to three numbers in turn, for example 30, 40, 70. The other children then add these. *What method did you use?* If necessary, remind children that they can use $7 + 3 = 10$ to work out $70 + 30 = 100$. How many different ways can they find of making 140 with three darts?

- Put children into pairs and give each pair a set of number cards for the multiples of 10 from 20 to 90. The first player turns over three cards and adds the numbers. Their partner checks the total. If the answer is correct the first player collects a counter, and they swap roles.

Feedback

Can each child:

- partition numbers into tens and units, adding the tens first?
- add three two-digit multiples of 10?

Does anyone not use, for example, $3 + 4 = 7$ to work out $30 + 40 = 70$?

Can children explain/record informally how they added three two-digit numbers?

Objective

Develop written methods for subtraction of whole numbers less than 1000.

Resources

▸ none needed

What children are learning

a written method for subtracting numbers which are too large to subtract mentally
to approximate before calculating

Words you can use

minus, subtract, take away, difference between, check, plus, add

Things to note

▸ Children will naturally approximate before calculating to give themselves an idea of
  whether the answer they are considering is likely. Approximating calculations is a
  very important skill to develop.
▸ Children should be able to subtract any two-digit numbers mentally before being
  introduced to standard written methods for subtraction.
▸ These activities allow children to work in whichever way is appropriate for them.
  This may involve working mentally and making informal jottings, for example:

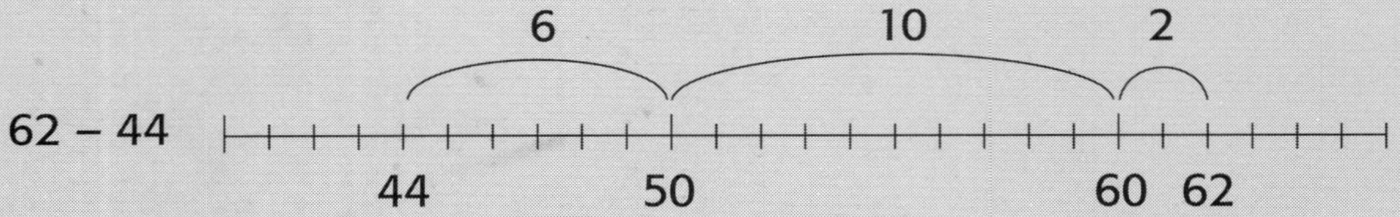

or using a more formal method, for example:

$$\begin{array}{r} 62 \\ -\,44 \\ \hline \end{array} \quad \begin{array}{r} 50 + 12 \\ -\,40 + 4 \\ \hline 10 + 8 \end{array} = 18$$

Activities

❶ Develop written methods for subtraction of whole numbers less than 1000.

▸ Write about twelve single- and two-digit numbers on the board, for example 36, 9, 56, 73, 4, 62, 27, 44, 97, 13, 7, 81. Ask the children to work in pairs or groups of three. They have three or four minutes to subtract whichever numbers they choose to get as close as possible to a target number. *I'm going to set you a target number. Choose two numbers and find the difference between them to get as close to the target number as you can. The first target number is 50.*

$$\begin{array}{rcrcr} 81 & = & 70 & + & 11 \\ -\,27 & & -\,20 & + & 7 \\ \hline & & 50 & + & 4 & = & 54 \end{array} \qquad \begin{array}{rcrcr} 62 & = & 50 & + & 12 \\ -\,13 & & -\,10 & + & 3 \\ \hline & & 40 & + & 9 & = & 49 \end{array}$$

The children in each group compare their answers and the child whose answer is nearest to the target wins a counter. A second counter can be awarded if the target number is made exactly. Alternatively, the winner can announce the target for the next round, which should be between 0 and 100. Further targets can include 50, 25, 61 etc.

▸ Set different tasks, including winning a counter for:
 – reaching a total between 30 and 40 or between 15 and 20
 – finding which two numbers have a difference of 26 (62 – 36)
 – finding a difference of 29 in two different ways, for example 73 – 44 and 56 – 27.

▸ *Variation:* three-digit numbers can be introduced if appropriate. Write 359, 72, 212, 17, 434, 61, 32, 70, 159, 8 on the board. Targets might include finding two numbers with a difference as close as possible to 150, 200, 250 etc., a number between 140 and 160, between 80 and 90 etc.

Feedback

Can each child:
▸ subtract whole numbers less than 100 using a written method?
▸ subtract whole numbers less than 1000 using a written method?

When using a vertical layout, can children explain each step of the calculation?

Is anyone making mistakes where the units digit of the number being subtracted is larger than the units digit of the start number, for example 91 – 47?

Money and 'real-life' problems

Objective

Choose appropriate number operations and calculation methods to solve money and 'real-life' word problems with one or more steps.

Resources

- cards made from **PCM 3**
- additional cards if necessary (see Things to note)

What children are learning

- to solve word problems in real-life situations
- to explain how they worked out a word problem

Words you can use

solve, problem, add, subtract, multiply, divide, methods, greater than, less than, equal to

Things to note

- The numbers on the cards on **PCM 3** can be masked and altered to provide a greater number of problems to solve, including those with larger numbers to provide more of a challenge. For example, the numbers on the card reading 'A postman delivers 16 parcels on Monday and 17 on Tuesday. How many parcels does he deliver?' can be altered to 25 and 38. Similarly, smaller numbers can be used if more appropriate for the children.
- Some children may struggle to read the worded problems. If necessary, work together as a group, reading each question aloud and asking the children to write the number sentence and answer.
- It is sometimes useful for children to draw or model a situation, for example collecting sixteen and seventeen cubes to stand for parcels and counting the total number.
- In this activity, discussion of *how* to solve the problem is more important than actually calculating the answer. Encourage children to discuss possible methods in depth. It is better to look at one or two problems in detail than to skim through a lot of problems.

Activities

❶ **Solve word problems in real-life situations.**

- Spread out the cards made from **PCM 3**. Choose a card to discuss as a group. Encourage children to focus on and discuss the methods that they would use to solve the problem rather than on finding the answer. Ask them to jot down how they could work it out. Explore different vocabulary and ensure that children have developed a picture of the problem.

This will help them to decide which operation to use and how to calculate this answer. Discuss several problems in this way before moving on.

▸ Ask the children to choose a card each and try to read the problem. *What does your card say? What do you have to work out? What would you do to find this answer? How could you work it out?* Ask children to write the answer they have found on the back of their card. Discuss each child's problem in turn with the group and ask them to suggest how it could be solved. *Do you think this is an addition question? Would you take away to find the answer? How did you do the addition/ subtraction/multiplication? What do you think the answer is?* Children can all say what they think the answer is. If they agree with the answer written on the back of the card, the child whose card it is can collect a counter. Ask the children to pick another card each and repeat the process.

▸ Once all the cards have been explored in this way, write several number sentences on the board involving all four operations, for example 24 + 13, 21 − 14, 15 × 4, 55 ÷ 5 etc. Ask each child in turn to make up a problem based around these number sentences, for example 'Jamie had £24 and was given £13 for his birthday, how much money has he got now?' All the children in the group should try to work out the answer and write it down. The child who made up the question should say which number sentence the question was based on, how the answer could be found and then give the answer. These problems could be recorded on paper for future use.

Feedback

Can each child:
▸ solve worded problems in real-life situations?
▸ explain how they worked out a problem?

Can children identify a real-life situation that gives rise to a maths problem?

Which children could break down a two-step problem and explain their method?

Objective

Count back in equal steps including below zero.

Resources

▸ ⁻30–30 number line
▸ copies of **PCM 4**
▸ counters

What children are learning

▸ to count back in equal steps from any number including below zero
▸ to create and describe simple number sequences

Words you can use

count on, count back, equal, steps, multiple, zero, number, sequence, pattern, difference, more, less, tens, units, minus, negative

Things to note

▸ Counting forwards and backwards in different sized steps helps children to gain an understanding of how numbers relate to each other. Children build up a mental picture of where numbers are, and over time are able to visualize how many more or less a number is than another without needing to count.
▸ Counting on in steps of a constant size can help children to answer addition and subtraction questions without the need to count, for example 14 + 7 can be answered by knowing that seven more than fourteen is twenty-one. The ability to count on and back can help children to recognize, continue and explain number sequences more easily, for example 3, 7, 11, 15 …
▸ Refer to ⁻1, ⁻2 etc. as 'minus one', 'minus two' etc. and describe these numbers collectively as 'negative numbers'.

Activities

❶ **Count back in equal steps including to less than zero.**

▸ Before copying **PCM 4**, write the following numbers in the frogs (these can be simplified if too difficult for the children in the group)

3   3   4   4   5   5   6   6   10   10

and write a small two-digit start number in the first lily pad on each line, for example 23, 17, 19 etc.

Give each child a copy of the PCM and ask them to fill in numbers on the lily-pad trails by counting back in steps of the size shown in each frog. Children may need to count back on a ⁻30–30 number line using a counter, for example moving back three jumps at a time. Discuss the patterns that children find. *What do you notice about counting back in threes? Can you say these numbers? What do you call this number? Have you seen a pattern that can help you to find the next number without counting or using the number line?* (for example, counting back in tens: ⁻13, ⁻23, ⁻33 etc.) Ask the children to extend these sequences as far as they can.

- Once the lily-pad trails have been filled in, children should check their answers with a friend's by counting their numbers aloud in pairs. Any differences between their answers can be checked with the rest of the group. The numbers could be read from right to left in order to practise counting forwards in steps of a constant size.
- Children can then cover some of their numbers with counters. In pairs, children can work out the hidden numbers on their sequences.

  Variation: children can check their sequences using the 'constant function' on a calculator, for example key in the following to check the first sequence:

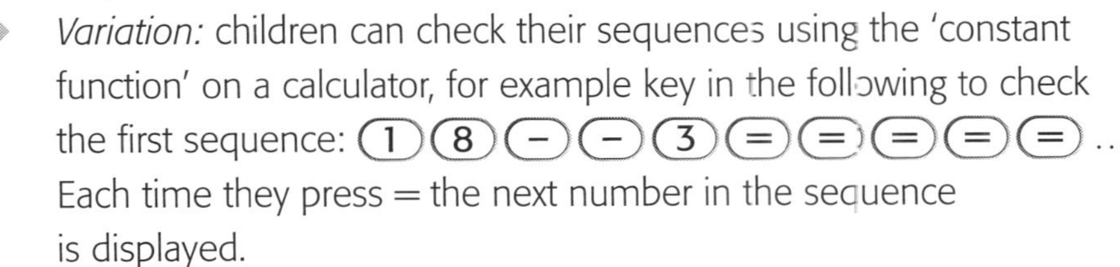

  Each time they press = the next number in the sequence is displayed.

Feedback

Can each child:
- count back in equal steps from any number including below zero?
- create and describe simple number sequences?

Which children spotted and explained patterns in the sequences?

Can all children successfully add/subtract a small number when going over zero, for example 'add three to minus one', or 'count back five from two'?

Mental calculation strategies (+ and –)

Objective

Add/subtract 2 two-digit numbers (crossing 10 but not 100 boundary).

Resources

- counters in two colours
- sets of 1–50 and 0–100 number cards
- 100 squares

What children are learning

- to mentally add 2 two-digit numbers (crossing 10 but not 100 boundary), for example 34 + 59
- to mentally subtract 2 two-digit numbers (crossing 10 but not 100 boundary), for example 67 – 48

Words you can use

plus, add, total, altogether, more, take away, subtract, minus, equals, makes

Things to note

- The idea that the position of a digit in a number determines its worth is known as 'place value'. Place value in our number system allows us to create an infinite series of numbers using just ten digits (0, 1, 2, 3, 4, 5, 6, 7, 8 and 9). Place-value cards can help children to appreciate that the 1 in the number 17 is worth 10 etc.
- Use the range of vocabulary listed above so that children experience more than one way of describing addition, for example 'three plus five', 'three and five', 'three add five', 'the total of three and five', 'three and five altogether' etc. Similarly, children need to hear and use a variety of subtraction vocabulary.
- Encourage children to look carefully at the numbers in the calculation and to decide which strategy to use to add/subtract. They should have a range of strategies to choose from for both addition and subtraction.

Activities

❶ Add/subtract 2 two-digit numbers.

1	2	3	4	5	6	7	8	9	10
11	12	◯	14	15	16	17	18	19	20
21	22	23	24	25	26	27	28	29	30
31	32	33	34	35	36	37	38	39	40
41	42	43	44	45	46	47	48	49	50
51	52	53	54	55	56	57	58	59	60
61	62	63	64	65	66	67	68	69	70
71	72	73	74	75	76	77	78	79	80
◯	82	83	84	85	86	87	88	89	90
91	92	93	94	95	96	97	98	99	100

▸ Children play this game in pairs; each pair needs counters in two colours, a set of 1–50 number cards and a 100 square between them. The first player turns over two cards, for example 34 and 47. They add the numbers (to make 81 in this case) and subtract the numbers (making 13) and put counters of their colour on both numbers. The cards are replaced at the bottom of the pack, which should be shuffled occasionally. Play then passes to the second child. The winner is the first player to get three counters in a line vertically, horizontally or diagonally.

▸ *Variation:* children can play the game as above but instead of putting a counter on the results of both the addition and subtraction questions, they decide which of the two answers offers most advantage and place just one counter in each turn. This version will obviously take longer to play.

▸ This game is called 'Nearest to fifty' and can be played with any number of players from two to the whole group. Each player turns over two cards from a set of 0–100 number cards. They can decide whether to add or subtract the numbers towards making an answer that is as close as possible to fifty. For example, a child who turns over 34 and 21 should decide to add, making a total of 55 (subtracting would result in 13); a child who turns over 87 and 42 should subtract, resulting in 45. All the answers are compared and the child whose answer is nearest to fifty wins a counter. Encourage the children to check the winning calculation.

Feedback

Can each child:

▸ add 2 two-digit numbers (crossing 10 but not 100 boundary)?
▸ subtract 2 two-digit numbers (crossing 10 boundary)?

Did children find approximate answers to help them check whether their answer could be correct?

Is anyone regularly making the mistake of subtracting by taking the smaller digit from the larger, regardless of its place value, for example '71 − 24 = 53'?

Rapid recall of number facts (+ and −)

Objective

Derive addition pairs that total 100, multiples of 50 that total 1000.

Resources

- large 100 square
- 0–100 number cards
- number cards for the multiples of 50 to 1000
- extra 500-card

What children are learning

- pairs of numbers to 100 that add to 100, for example 35 + 65, 82 + 18 etc.
- pairs of multiples of 50 that add to 1000, for example 150 + 850, 300 + 700

Words you can use

pair, total, add, plus, equals, makes, multiple

Things to note

- The learning of number facts is an ongoing process throughout the year. This lesson could be repeated several times during the year to provide practice and assessment of the addition facts children are required to learn.
- Describe addition and subtraction questions using a range of vocabulary, including words like 'altogether', 'sum', 'total', 'plus', 'add', 'and', 'more than', 'subtract', 'take away', 'take', 'difference between', 'minus' etc.
- Children will need to know pairs of multiples of 5 that add to 100 in order to derive multiples of 50 that total 1000, for example 15 + 85 = 100 and 150 + 850 = 1000.
- Children often make the mistake of saying 71 + 39 = 100 because they look at the multiples of 10 to total 100, ignoring the units.

Activities

❶ **Derive addition pairs that total 100.**

- Use a large 100 square and a set of 0–100 number cards. Children take turns to take a card, for example 36, and place it on the number that would add to it to make 100 (64 in this case). How quickly can all the cards be placed?

- Practise number facts to 100 in a 'target quiz': you say a number, for example 34; the first child to say the 'partner to 100' (66 in this case) wins a point. If a child correctly answers two consecutive questions they can give the next number. If children are unsure, use the 100 square to check, for example *Start at thirty-six. How many do we jump to get to forty?* (4) *How many do we jump to get from forty to one hundred?* (60)

  Variation: children can begin by finding partners to 30 and 50 if necessary.

❷ **Recall pairs of multiples of 50 that make 1000.**
Spread the cards showing the multiples of 50 face down on the table, together with an extra 500-card (to make a 500 + 500 pair). Children take turns to turn over two cards, one at a time. If the numbers add to 1000 the child keeps the pair and says the number sentence aloud, for example 'four hundred and fifty plus five hundred and fifty equals one thousand'. If the numbers do not add to 1000, the child replaces the cards face

down and play passes to the next child. Encourage children to remember where certain numbers have been replaced to help them to form future totals of 1000. *What number have you turned over? So what number do you need to make 1000? Have you seen that number anywhere?* The game continues until all the pairs to 1000 have been made. If children are having difficulty, draw their attention to the relationship between pairs of numbers that make 10 and 100, for example $6 + 4 = 10$, $60 + 40 = 100$. Extend this to show that $600 + 400 = 1000$. Similarly, help children to see the link between $35 + 65 = 100$ and $350 + 650 = 1000$.

Feedback

Can each child:

- derive addition pairs that total 100?
- derive multiples of 50 that total 1000?

Who could explain that they knew $400 + 600 = 1000$ because they know that $6 + 4 = 10$?

Does anyone regularly give the pair that make 110, rather than 100, because they are looking only at the tens columns, for example saying $78 + 32 = 100$?

Reasoning about numbers

Objectives

Investigate general statements about familiar numbers.
Explain methods and reasoning.

Resources

▸ calculators

What children are learning

to explore statements about familiar numbers, for example odd and even numbers,
and give examples that match them

Words you can use

odd, even, answer, multiple, digit, pattern

Things to note

▸ A 'multiple' is a number that another divides into without a remainder, for example
multiples of 2 are numbers that when divided by two have no remainder. Children
may learn multiples as 'answers to the times tables', for example multiples of 2 are
the answers to the 2 times table. However, it is important that children realize that
numbers beyond the times table can also be multiples, for example multiples of 2
include numbers beyond 20, such as 68 and 432.

▸ Ask questions that encourage children to explain the patterns they notice and to
predict further solutions to the problem, for example *What do you notice? How do
you know whether you have found all the ways? Can you see any patterns in the
numbers? Explain this to the others.* Try to encourage all children to explain their
thinking. Where possible, children could begin to write a simple explanation of the
pattern in words.

Activities

❶ **Investigate general statements.**

▸ Begin by writing the following sentence on the board:
'Multiples of … end in … '
In a different colour write the number 5 into the first space.
Give each child a calculator and ask them to key in ⓪ ⊕ ⊕ ⑤ ⊜ ⊜ …
(or to enter + 5 = each time). Each time the equals key is pressed the display will
add on in fives from zero, for example 0, 5, 10, 15, 20, 25, 30 … Remind children
that these numbers are 'multiples of 5'.

Ask the children to write down some of the numbers and label them. *What do these numbers have in common? How can you recognize a multiple of five?* Discuss that multiples of 5 end in 0 or 5. Ask children to copy the sentence from the board and fill in the last space.

Multiples of 5

10, 25, 5, 30, 45

▸ Now alter the sentence to read 'Multiples of 10 end in …' and ask children to copy and complete the sentence. *What do all multiples of ten end in? How can you recognize a multiple of ten?*

▸ Change the number 10 in the sentence to 2, then 4, then 8 etc. and ask children to copy and complete the sentences in the same way. Encourage children to generate sequences of multiples by using the calculator, for example ⓪ ⊕ ⊕ ② ⊜ ⊜ … for multiples of 2 or ⓪ ⊕ ⊕ ④ ⊜ ⊜ … for multiples of 4 etc. Children should notice that all multiples of 2, 4 and 8 are even numbers that end with 0, 2, 4, 6, or 8.

▸ When multiples of 2, 4, 5, 8 and 10 have been explored and the sentences completed, children could explore multiples of 50 and 100 in this way, for example 'Multiples of 100 end in 00', 'Multiples of 50 end in 50 or 00'.

Feedback

Can each child:
▸ explore statements about multiples, and give examples that match them?
▸ make a general statement on the basis of several examples?

Who made comments about patterns they notice, for example 'all the multiples of 8 are also multiples of 4'?

Objective

Divide a whole number of £ by 2, 4, 5 or 10 to give £·p.

Resources

▸ cards marked '÷ 2', '÷ 4', '÷ 5', '÷ 10'
▸ £1, 50p and 10p coins

What children are learning

▸ when we divide we create equal sets
▸ how to divide whole pounds to give an answer in pounds or in pence

Words you can use

divide, share, equals, makes, pound, pence, sign

Things to note

▸ Never use both a pound sign and a pence sign when recording an amount. If a decimal point is used it should be in conjunction with the pound sign only, for example £5·24 (never £5·24p).
▸ Children need to appreciate that when we divide we form *equal* sets.
▸ Division can be thought of as equal sharing or equal grouping. Equal sharing, which is the focus of the activities below, can be done by a 'one for me, one for you' approach, continually equalizing the numbers in the sets. Equal grouping, on the other hand, can be thought of as continually subtracting groups of a number from the original number.

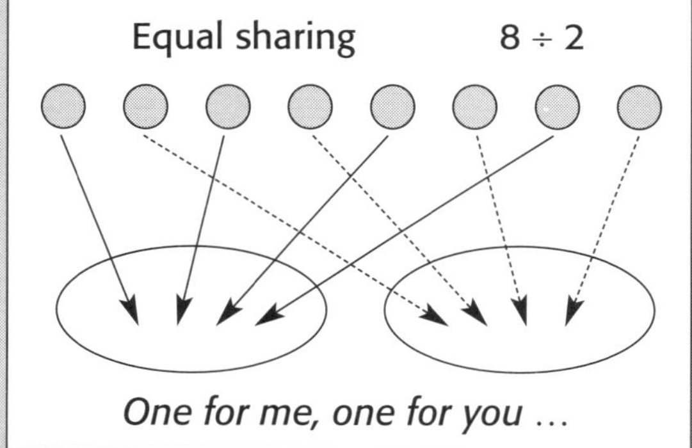

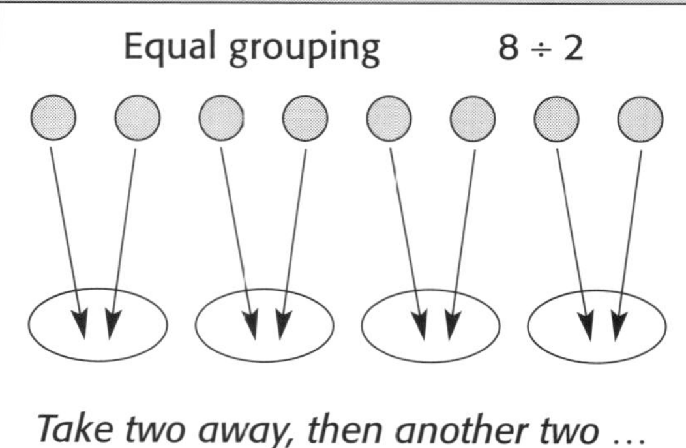

▸ If children find sharing between four difficult, encourage them to share between two and then split each of the two groups in half, making four equal groups.

Activities

❶ Divide a whole number of pounds by 2, 4, 5 or 10 to give £ and p.

▸ You will need cards marked '÷ 2', '÷ 4', '÷ 5', '÷ 10' for this activity. Give each child ten £1 coins. Children take turns to pick a card, for example ÷ 2. They then split their money into that many equal sets, for example into two sets. Encourage children to think of this as how many people the money is to be shared between: *Ten pounds shared between two people equals five pounds each* or *Ten pounds divided by two equals five pounds*. Demonstrate how this can be written as a number sentence: £10 ÷ 2 = £5.

If the answer to a division is not in whole pounds (for example, £10 ÷ 4) show the child how to exchange the remaining two £1 coins for four 50p coins, which can then be shared out between the four groups. This should be recorded as £10 ÷ 4 = £2·50.

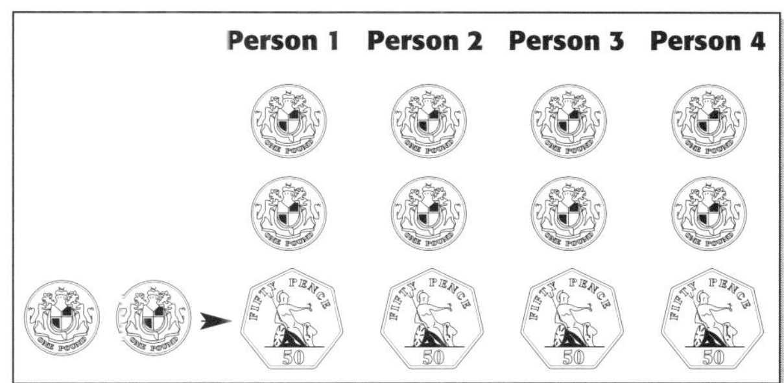

▸ Once £10 has been shared between 2, 4, 5 or 10 and number sentences recorded, each child should give you back one £1 coin, leaving them with nine pounds as their start number. Children should continue to take turns to pick a card and divide their amount of money by the number on the card. Children will need to swap their £1 coins for smaller coins to answer some of the questions. *How would you describe this? How would you write this as a number sentence?*

▸ Continue the activity for £8, £7, £6, £5 … in the same way. Where answers are smaller than one pound, encourage children to record amounts in pence, for example £8 ÷ 10 = 80p.

	Person									
	1	2	3	4	5	6	7	8	9	10
£8 ⟶	80p	80p	80p	80p	80p	80p	80p	80p	80p	80p

Feedback

Can each child:

▸ divide amounts of money by sharing into equal sets?

▸ divide whole pounds to give an answer in pounds or in pence?

Is everyone confident about swapping remaining money into smaller units so that it can be shared?

Objective

Use closely related facts, for example derive ×9 or ×11 from ×10, or derive ×6 from ×4 plus ×2.

Resources

▸ sets of 1–20 cards
▸ operation cards showing '9 ×', '10 ×' and '11 ×'
▸ calculators

What children are learning

▸ to find 9× a number by first finding 10× and then subtracting the number
▸ to find 11× a number by first finding 10× and then adding the number

Words you can use

multiply, times, lots of, groups of, equals, makes, add, plus, subtract, minus, take away

Things to note

▸ Children often have difficulty filling in the tables used in these activities. You may need to show how the number at the start of the row is multiplied by the number at the top of each column.
▸ Remind children that multiplication can be done in any order, for example 11×5 gives the same answer as 5×11.
▸ Avoid telling children to 'add a zero' when multiplying by ten. Instead discuss that the digits move across into the next column, for example for 10×7 the 7 in the units column becomes seven tens and a zero is placed in the units column.
▸ Children need to be able to multiply by ten to use the strategies covered in this unit.
▸ It is often helpful to explain strategies with practical examples, for example 'I want to find out what eleven videos would cost at £12 each. I know that ten would cost £120, so eleven must cost £12 more, which is £132'.

Activities

❶ **Derive ×9 or ×11 from ×10.**

▸ Draw this grid on the board or on a large sheet of paper. Explain that you are going to fill the spaces in the grid by multiplying the number at the start of the row by the number at the top of each column.

×	5	8	9	12	14	16	21
9							
10							
11							

Complete the 10× row first, then move on to the 11× row. *We know that ten times five is fifty. So how can we find eleven times five? That's the same as ten times five add one more lot of five. So that's fifty plus five, which is fifty-five.* Ask children to complete the 11× row. Write further numbers along the top as children become more confident. *If we know ten times a number, how can we find eleven times?* Children should be able to tell you that you find ten times the number and then add one more lot of the number.

▸ Introduce 9× in the same way. *If we know ten times a number, how can we find nine times? Let's work out the first one, which is nine times five. We know that ten times five is fifty so to find nine times five we take off one lot of five. So that's fifty minus five, which is forty-five.* Children can then work across the 9× row.

▸ Give each pair of children a set of 1–20 cards, and several of each of the operation cards ('9 ×', '10 ×' and '11 ×') and a calculator. Shuffle each set of cards and place them in separate piles face down. Player 1 turns over one of the operation cards, for example 11 ×, and one of the number cards, for example 14. They keep the card if they can correctly answer the sum ($11 \times 14 = 154$). Player 2 checks on the calculator. The 11 × card is returned to the bottom of the pile of operation cards. Allow children to make jottings on paper to work out the answers.

▸ Ask *How could we find twelve times a number?* Demonstrate that to find 12× we can find 10× the number and then add two more lots of the number, for example $12 \times 15 = (10 \times 15) + (2 \times 15) = 150 + 30 = 180$.

▸ *How could we find eight times a number?* Show that we can find 8× by finding 10× the number and then subtracting two lots of the number, for example $8 \times 15 = (10 \times 15) - (2 \times 15) = 150 - 30 = 120$.

Feedback

Can each child:

▸ work out 10× a number?
▸ work out 9× a number by first finding 10×?
▸ work out 11× a number by first finding 10×?
▸ work out 12× a number by first finding 10×?
▸ work out 8× a number by first finding 10×?

Does anyone have difficulty explaining the process used in these strategies, for example 14×11 (they can use jottings)?

Pencil and paper procedures (× and ÷)

Objectives

Partition and multiply.
Develop and refine written methods for TU × U.

Resources

▸ none needed

What children are learning

a pencil and paper method of multiplication which uses place value and lets children see clearly how multiplication works

Words you can use

times, multiply, multiplied by, partition, total, product

Things to note

▸ To use the methods covered in this lesson children need to be able to partition or split numbers into tens and units and to multiply a single-digit number by a multiple of 10 (for example 7 × 40).

▸ Children should be confident with using the 'grid' or 'area' method of multiplication before moving towards a more standard method. If necessary, spend time developing the necessary competence with these informal methods before moving on. It is better that children continue to use a method they understand and are successful with than to rush them on to a new way they don't understand.

▸ Both the grid method and the standard method use partitioning and place value.

▸ The standard method can be seen as a shortcut of the grid method if the links between the two are made.

▸ The idea that the position of a digit in a number determines its worth is known as 'place value', so even though the two fives in 5357 look the same, they are worth different amounts. Place-value cards can help children to appreciate that the first 5 is worth five thousand whereas the second 5 is worth fifty.

Activities

❶ **Partition and multiply.**

▸ Write some two-digit numbers on the board, for example 34, 72, 59, and ask children to split, or partition, the numbers into tens and units, for example 30 + 4, 70 + 2 and 50 + 9. Ensure children can do this before moving on.

▸ Write a multiplication question on the board, for example 5 × 29, and show how to solve it using the grid method. Ask children to give an approximate answer first. Write further multiplication questions on the board for children to solve using the grid method, for example 26 × 4, 19 × 5, 32 × 6. Encourage children to approximate first to get a rough idea of the expected answer.

	20	9	
5	100	45	= 145

❷ **Develop and refine written methods for TU × U.**

▸ Choose a calculation, for example 27 × 5, and invite a child to solve it on the board using the grid method. Solve the question alongside using a standard method. Point out how each step is the same as a step in the grid method. Each step is shown in brackets to help children focus on the part of the calculation they are doing. *We are doing a shortcut way so we don't always have to draw the rectangles.*

	20	7	
5	100	35	= 135

$$\begin{array}{r} 27 \\ \times\ 5 \\ \hline 100 \\ 35 \\ \hline 135 \end{array}$$

(5×20)
(5×7)

▸ Write another calculation on the board, for example 38 × 6. Invite a child to draw a rectangle and to solve the problem using the grid method. As the first part is completed (6 × 30) and 180 is written in the box, show this part of the calculation in the standard method. Linking the two methods, step by step, can help children to see the relationship between them. At this stage children will usually work out the most significant digit first, so in this case they will work out 6 × 30 and then 6 × 8.

$$\begin{array}{r} 38 \\ \times\ 6 \\ \hline 180 \\ \hline \end{array}$$

(6×30)

Feedback

Can each child:
▸ multiply single-digit numbers by multiples of 10?
▸ partition and multiply using an informal method, for example the grid method?
▸ use a standard method of multiplication?

Which children can confidently use the grid method, explaining each step?
If children are using a vertical layout, can they talk through what they are doing at each step?

Objectives

Choose appropriate number operations and calculation methods to solve money and real-life problems with one or more steps.
Explain working.

Resources

▸ cards made from **PCM 6**

What children are learning

to work out which operation to use when answering money problems and to explain their working

Words you can use

sort, set, coins, 1p, 2p, 5p, 10p, 20p, 50p, £1, £2, pound, pence, penny, how many?, total, cost, pay, price, count, number, more, fewer, altogether, left, subtract, change, addition, subtraction, multiplication, division, expensive, cheaper

Things to note

▸ When describing worded problems involving money, use a range of vocabulary, for example *How much is that altogether? What will it cost? What will the total cost be? How much money would you need? How much more/less is that? How much would you have left? What change would you be given?*

▸ Never use both a pound sign and a pence sign when recording an amount. If a decimal point is used it should be in conjunction with the pound sign only, for example £5·24 (never £5·24p).

▸ When solving worded problems, children often find it difficult to decide whether to add, subtract, multiply or divide. Avoid just telling them what to do. Encourage other children to explain the problem in their own words and to record the method using informal jottings. At this stage children are not expected to set questions out in a formal way, for example using vertical columns. Instead children should be encouraged to write horizontally, using notation they are comfortable with.

▸ Children sometimes become confused when prices are written in different ways, for example £2 + £4·15 or £3·20 + 95p. Encourage them to rewrite the question into the same form, for example £2·00 + £4·15 and £3·20 + £0·95.

Activities

❶ Solve problems involving money.

Invite each child to pick two of the cards made from **PCM 6** and place them face up on the table.

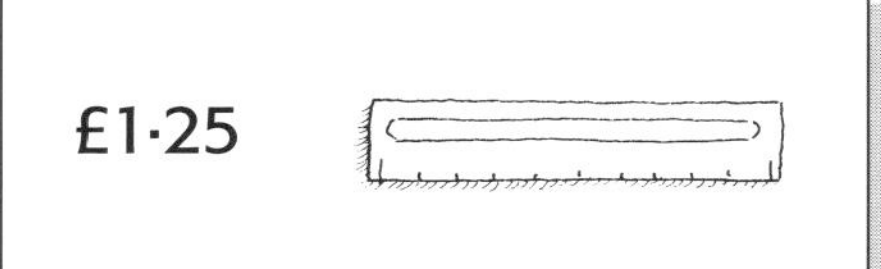

Ask some general questions about the items on the cards, for example *Who has the cheapest item? How much does it cost? Which is the most expensive item? What price is it?* Then begin to ask more specific questions about the items, and ask children to write down their answers on paper. For each invite children to explain which operation they would use (*Would you use addition, subtraction, multiplication, or division?*) and to record the question and answer as a number statement, for example £2 + £4·35 = £6·35. Include questions from the following list:

- *What is the total cost of your two items?*
- *Which coins could you use to pay for these two items exactly?*
- *If you paid with a £10 note, how much change would you get?*
- *What is the difference between your two prices?*
- *Choose one of your cards. If you bought two of this item, how much would you spend?*
- *How much would it cost to buy (ten) of this item?* (Children may find this difficult if they have to multiply a decimal by 10, for example £4·25 × 10.)
- *How many of this item could you buy with £5?*

Encourage children to make jottings to support their method and to explain their working to the rest of the group.

▶ *Variation:* if children have difficulty with adding, subtracting, multiplying and dividing, select appropriate cards to give to them, rather than letting them choose, for example provide them with the following cards: tin of beans 40p, milk 48p. This will enable them to concentrate on deciding *what to do* rather than on the difficulty of the calculations.

Feedback

Can each child:

▸ work out which operation to use when answering money problems?
▸ explain their working?

What methods are children using to calculate change? Are they consistently correct? (When buying something for £6·50 with £10, children will often say that the change is £4·50 because 4 + 6 = 10.)

Do children approximate the answer to the question before working it out?

Objectives

Recognize equivalence of simple fractions.
Compare a fraction with one-half, and say whether it is greater or less.

Resources

- copy of **PCM 7** for each child
- dice marked $\frac{1}{2}, \frac{1}{4}, \frac{1}{4}, \frac{1}{8}, \frac{1}{8}, \frac{1}{8}$
- dice marked $\frac{1}{2}, \frac{1}{3}, \frac{1}{4}, \frac{1}{6}, \frac{1}{12}, \frac{1}{12}$
- equal-length strips of paper marked into halves, quarters or tenths
- two hoops
- fraction cards (for example, $\frac{3}{4}, \frac{5}{6}, \frac{3}{8}, \frac{5}{8}, \frac{7}{8}, \frac{2}{3}, \frac{1}{3}, \frac{3}{10}, \frac{7}{10}, \frac{1}{5}, \frac{4}{5}$ etc.)

What children are learning

- that fractions are equal parts of things
- that some fractions are equivalent
- how to compare fractions

Words you can use

fraction, half, quarter, divide, whole, equal, parts

Things to note

- Equivalent fractions are the same part of a whole, for example $\frac{1}{2} = \frac{2}{4}$.
- When children first encounter fractions in school, it is usually in relation to areas of shapes, for example half of a circle, one-quarter of a square etc. Children often build up a visual picture of these fractions without realizing the significance of the notation, for example that $\frac{1}{2}$ means one out of two equal parts.
- As children's understanding of fractions grows, they will begin to realize that any number, shape or set of objects can be split into equal parts to make fractions. For example, twenty can be split into four equal parts to make quarters; each of the quarters is worth five.
- Fractions can be represented in different ways, for example two halves needn't look the same as long as they are the same size, as here:

- Children may need experience of equivalent fractions in a range of contexts if they are to realize that, for example, $\frac{5}{10}$ and $\frac{1}{2}$ are equivalent.

Activities

❶ Recognize equivalence of simple fractions.

▸ Give each pair of children two copies of **PCM 7** and a dice marked $\frac{1}{2}, \frac{1}{4}, \frac{1}{4}, \frac{1}{8}, \frac{1}{8}, \frac{1}{8}$. The players take turns to roll the dice and colour the fraction on one of the pizzas. They don't need to colour a pizza completely before beginning another but they must only colour parts of one pizza during each turn. The winner is the first player to colour all the pizzas. (You may need to reinforce that $\frac{1}{4}$ of a pizza is two slices.)

▸ Children can play the game again but this time using a dice marked $\frac{1}{2}, \frac{1}{3}, \frac{1}{4}, \frac{1}{6}, \frac{1}{12}, \frac{1}{12}$ and colouring in the flags on the second part of the PCM.

❷ Compare a fraction with one-half, and say whether it is greater or less.

▸ Show children each of the strips of paper in turn. For each ask *What fraction is this strip split into? How do you know? This one is split into tenths because there are ten equal pieces.*

▸ Count along the tenths strip: *One tenth, two tenths … three tenths* recording the fractions on the board as you count. (You could ask a child to do this.)

▸ Blu-tack the three strips on the board, one above the other.

0		$\frac{1}{2}$		1

0	$\frac{1}{4}$	$\frac{1}{2}$	$\frac{3}{4}$	$\frac{4}{4}$

0	$\frac{1}{10}$	$\frac{2}{10}$	$\frac{3}{10}$	$\frac{4}{10}$	$\frac{5}{10}$	$\frac{6}{10}$	$\frac{7}{10}$	$\frac{8}{10}$	$\frac{9}{10}$	$\frac{10}{10}$

Is seven tenths bigger or smaller than one-half? How do you know? (It is further to the right.) *Can you tell me some other fractions that are bigger than one-half?*

▸ Place two hoops on the table, labelled as shown. Children take turns to take a card from the pile of fraction cards and place it in the appropriate hoop. *What do you notice about two-quarters? Why can't you put it in either of the hoops? It is the same size as one-half. Is any other fraction equal to one-half? If you could choose five-tenths or one-half of a bar of chocolate, which would you choose? Why?*

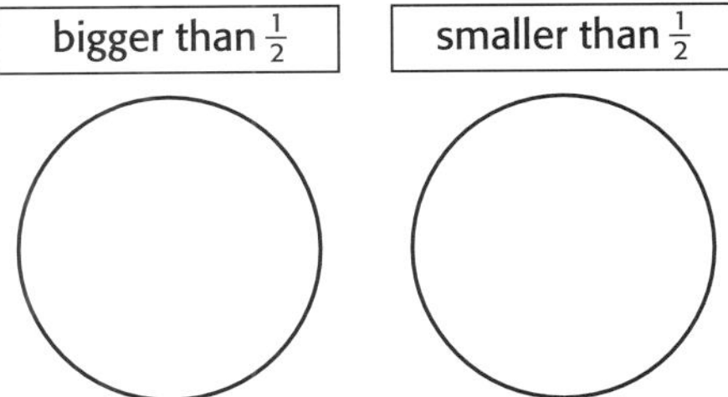

Feedback

Can each child:

▸ recognize equivalent fractions?

▸ compare a fraction with one-half, and say whether it is greater or less?

Does everyone realize that five-tenths and one-half of a bar of chocolate are the same?

Objective

Identify two fractions with a total of 1.

Resources

- interlocking cubes
- squared paper

What children are learning

- that fractions are equal parts of things
- to identify two fractions that together make a whole, for example $\frac{2}{5}$ and $\frac{3}{5}$

Words you can use

fraction, divide, whole, equal, parts, add, whole, half, quarter, fifth, eighth etc.

Things to note

- When children first encounter fractions in school, it is usually in relation to areas of shapes, for example $\frac{1}{4}$ of a circle, $\frac{1}{8}$ of a square etc. Children often build up a visual picture of these fractions without realizing the significance of the notation, for example that $\frac{1}{4}$ means one out of four equal parts. Children who do not understand this have difficulty recognizing that $\frac{1}{4}$ and $\frac{3}{4}$ equal one whole.
- Fractions can be represented in different ways, for example two eighths needn't look the same as long as they are the same size, as here:

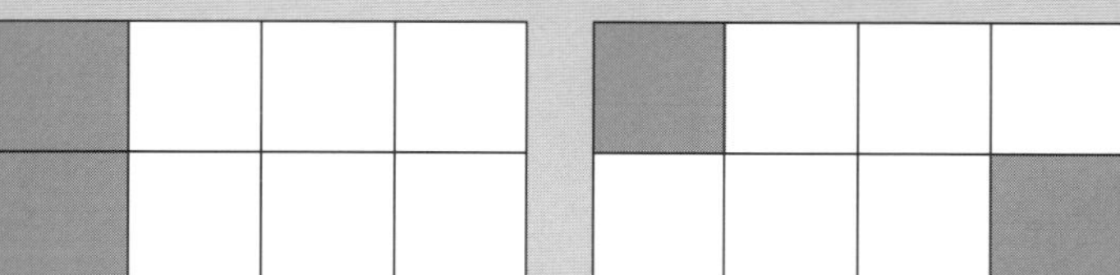

Activities

❶ Identify two fractions with a total of 1.

- Use four interlocking cubes to make a simple one-layer shape, as shown here:

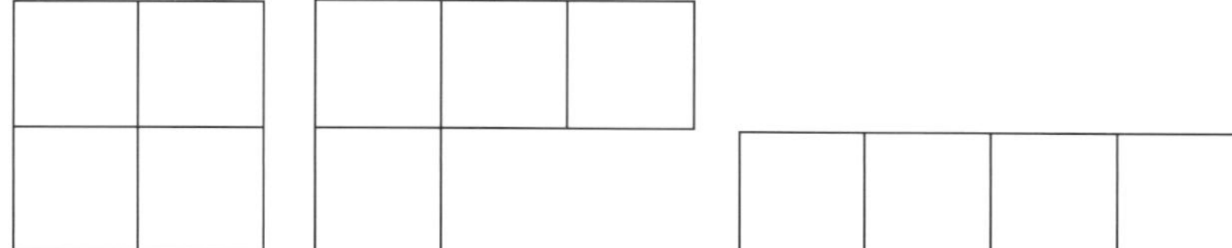

Pick up a single cube. *How many cubes are in this shape? Four. What fraction of the shape is one cube? One-quarter. How many more cubes do we need to make the whole shape? Three.* Add these cubes in a different colour to complete the shape. *What fraction of the whole shape is this? Three-quarters.*

▸ Ask the children to make a series of one-layer shapes. These can be drawn on squared paper. They then write the fraction that one cube is of the whole shape and the fraction needed to complete the whole shape. When children have completed three or four shapes, draw their attention to the number patterns involved, showing that the two fractions add up to a whole. *What do you notice about these two fractions? How many quarters make a whole? Four. How much is one cube? One-quarter. How much is left? Three-quarters. How much is one-quarter and three-quarters?* Continue for other fraction pairs the children have listed.

$\frac{1}{4}$	$\frac{3}{4}$
$\frac{1}{5}$	$\frac{4}{5}$
$\frac{1}{6}$	$\frac{5}{6}$
$\frac{1}{8}$	$\frac{7}{8}$
$\frac{1}{10}$	$\frac{9}{10}$

▸ Ask children to repeat the activities, this time asking *What fraction of the shape is two cubes? How many more cubes do we need to make the whole shape? What fraction of the whole shape is this?* Refer to the written fractions again, showing that the two fractions add up to a whole. If children find the layout of the table confusing, ask them to record the fractions underneath the shape drawn on paper, for example as $\frac{3}{4} + \frac{1}{4} = 1$ whole.

$\frac{1}{2}$	$\frac{1}{2}$
$\frac{2}{5}$	$\frac{3}{5}$
$\frac{2}{6}$	$\frac{4}{6}$
$\frac{2}{8}$	$\frac{6}{8}$
$\frac{2}{10}$	$\frac{8}{10}$

▸ Write some fractions on the board, for example $\frac{3}{5}$, $\frac{5}{8}$, $\frac{4}{10}$, and ask children to say the fraction that adds to make one whole.

Feedback

Can each child:

▸ identify two fractions with a total of one?

▸ tell you the fraction of the whole shape that is coloured? (For example, given , children will sometimes make the mistake of saying two-fifths.)

Fractions and decimals

Objective

Use decimal notation for tenths, and use in context.

Resources

▸ metre sticks, each marked with ten distinct sections

What children are learning

▸ to appreciate that the column to the right of the decimal point stands for tenths
▸ to describe and read decimals correctly

Words you can use

decimal, decimal point, tenths, digit, divide, whole, equal, parts

Things to note

▸ This lesson explores tenths of a metre. Hundredths can be introduced in the same way if children are able. The next lesson explores hundredths in more detail.
▸ When discussing tenths of a metre, show children that one metre has been split into ten equal sections and each section is called a tenth.

Activities

❶ **Use decimal notation for tenths (metres), and use in context.**

▸ Show the children a metre stick with ten distinct sections. Point to the zero end and tell the children that this is zero. Point to the other end. *How long is it from zero to here?* Encourage children to say that it is one metre or one hundred centimetres. Explain that in today's lesson all the measurements are going to be in metres. Point to the position one-tenth of the way along the metre stick (10 cm mark). *If the whole stick is one metre, how much of a metre is this?* Children may suggest it is 10 cm, but encourage them to notice that, if we are giving the measurement in metres, this is one-tenth of a metre.

- Ask the children to count aloud with you as you point to 0, 10 cm, 20 cm, 30 cm … etc. *Zero, one-tenth of a metre, two-tenths of a metre, three-tenths of a metre … one metre.* Count backwards in tenths from one metre to zero.
- Now write the following on the board: 0 m, 0·1 m, 0·2 m, 0·3 m … 0·9 m, 1 m. Remind children that the column to the right of the dot (decimal point) is called tenths. Again, ask children to count forwards and backwards in tenths as you point to the decimals on the board. *Zero, one-tenth of a metre, two-tenths of a metre … one metre.*
- Point to sections of the metre stick out of order and ask children to say how many tenths and to write these as decimals on paper.

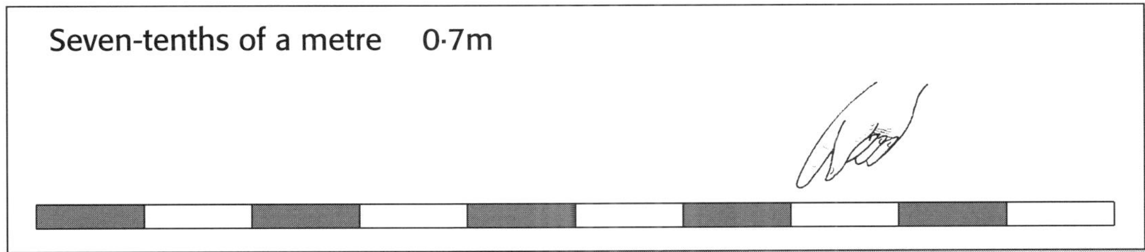

- Write some decimal measurements greater than one on the board or on a large sheet of paper, for example 1·3 m, 1·9 m, 2·1 m, 3·4 m, 3·8 m, 4·5 m. Explain that the number that comes before the dot (decimal point) tells us how many whole metres we have. Ask children to say these measurements aloud, for example 'One metre and three tenths of a metre'. Show this length using two metre sticks.

Feedback

Can each child:
- appreciate that the column to the right of the decimal point stands for tenths?
- describe and read decimals with tenths correctly?
- record seven tenths as 0·7?

Does any child have difficulty counting up in tenths from zero to one or from zero to three?

Do any children incorrectly say 'nought point eight, nought point nine, nought point *ten*'?

43 Fractions and decimals

Objectives

Use decimal notation for tenths, hundredths and use in context.
Convert metres to centimetres, and vice versa.

Resources

▸ a metre stick marked into 10 cm divisions

What children are learning

▸ to understand the tenths and hundredths columns, to the right of the decimal point
▸ to describe and read decimals correctly
▸ to convert measurements of length from metres to centimetres, and vice versa

Words you can use

decimal, decimal point, tenths, digit, divide, whole, equal, parts, convert

Things to note

▸ This lesson explores tenths and hundredths of metres. Children will need to have worked through activity sheet 42 before tackling this sheet.
▸ When discussing tenths of a metre, show children that one metre has been split into ten equal sections and that each section is called a tenth. When discussing hundredths of a metre, show children that one metre has been split into 100 equal sections and each section is called a hundredth.
▸ If appropriate, discuss the idea that 0·1 (one tenth) is the same as 0·10 (ten hundredths, or one tenth and zero hundredths). We can therefore describe 0·34 m as 'thirty-four hundredths of a metre' or 'three tenths and four hundredths of a metre'.
▸ Ensure that children say 'nought point two seven' not 'nought point twenty-seven' to describe 0·27 etc., describing each digit separately.

Activities

❶ **Use decimal notation for tenths, hundredths and use in context (metres).**

▸ Show a metre stick and point to the zero end. Tell the children that this is zero. Point to the other end and ask *How long is it from zero to here?* Encourage children to say that it is one metre or one hundred centimetres. Explain that in today's lesson all the measurements will be in metres. Revise tenths by pointing to the 10 cm, 20 cm, 30 cm … marks *out of order* and asking children to say how many tenths. Invite children to write these as decimals on the board.
▸ Introduce hundredths of a metre by pointing to the 1 cm mark. *There are one hundred of these equal parts in a metre, so we call this one hundredth of a metre.*

- Use base-10 sticks. *Each stick is one tenth of a metre* (0·1 m). Place them along the metre stick, counting as you go: *Nought point one, nought point two … .* (Discuss why one is not 'nought point ten' if children say this – *Ten tenths make one whole, in the same way that ten tens make one hundred.*)
- Place two base-10 sticks next to the metre stick. How much of a metre is this? (0·2) Place one cube next to it. *This is one hundredth of a metre. We now have two tenths and one hundredth. We write this as nought point two one.* Write 0·21 on the board under the column headings:

Wholes	·	tenths	hundredths
0	·	2	1

Show other amounts using base-10 apparatus in the same way, asking children to record these under the headings and to say each number aloud.
- Ask children to count with you in hundredths as you point to: 0, 1 cm, 2 cm … up to the 20 cm mark etc. *Zero, one hundredth of a metre, two hundredths of a metre, …* Show children that ten hundredths is the same as one tenth.

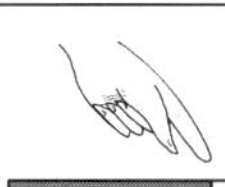

- Now write the following on the board: 0 m, 0·01 m, 0·02 m, 0·03 m, 0·04 m … 0·09 m, 0·10 m, 0·11 m … 0·20 m. Remind children that the columns to the right of the dot (decimal point) are called tenths and hundredths. Again, ask children to count forwards and backwards in hundredths as you point to the decimals on the board: *Zero, one hundredth of a metre … up to twenty hundredths (or two tenths).*

❷ Convert metres to centimetres, and vice versa.
- Write some other measurements on the board, for example 0·34 m, 0·64 m, 0·9 m, 0·88 m etc. Encourage the children to say these measurements aloud, for example 'thirty-four hundredths of a metre', and to point to these lengths on the metre stick. *How many centimetres are the same as thirty-four hundredths of a metre?* Encourage children to copy the decimals onto paper, writing them in a column down the page, and to write the equivalent measurement in centimetres next to each: 0·34 m = 34 cm. If children are confident, give them measurements in centimetres to convert to metres, for example 47 cm = 0·47 m.

Feedback

Can each child:
- understand the columns to the right of the decimal point (tenths and hundredths)?
- tell you the value of 3 in 2·34 m, for example?
- describe and read decimals correctly?
- convert measurements of length from metres to centimetres, and vice versa?

Which children can correctly convert 0·9 m to 90 cm?

Fractions and decimals

Objective

Order decimals with two places.

Resources

> metre sticks with clear 10 cm divisions
> **PCM 4**

What children are learning

> to understand the columns to the right of the decimal point, for example tenths and hundredths
> to describe and read decimals correctly
> to order two-digit decimals, for example 0·4, 0·7, 1·2, 3·8 …

Words you can use

decimal, decimal point, tenths, digit, divide, whole, equal, parts, convert

Things to note

> This lesson explores decimals with tenths, for example 0·4, 0·7, 1·2. Children will benefit from doing activity sheet 42 before this one.
> When discussing tenths of a metre, show children that one metre has been split into ten equal sections and that each section is called a tenth. When discussing hundredths of a metre, show children that one metre has been split into one hundred equal sections and that each section is called a hundredth.

Activities

❶ **Use decimal notation for tenths, hundredths and use in context (metres).**

> Show the children a metre stick and point to the zero end. Tell the children that this is zero. Point to the other end. *How long is it from zero to here?* Encourage children to say that it is one metre or one hundred centimetres. Explain that in today's lesson all the measurements will be in metres. Revise tenths by pointing *out of order* to the 10 cm marks (e.g. 10 cm, 90 cm …) along the number line and ask children to say and record the decimal, for example 0·1 m, 0·9 m, 0·7 m, 0·4 m etc. Remind children how measurements above one metre are written, for example 1·2 m, 2·5 m, 4·7 m etc.

> Ask children to count with you in steps of one-tenth from zero to beyond one: 0·1, 0·2 … 3·0 (or 4·0) etc. *Zero, nought point one, nought point two … one, one point one, one point two …* Point to positions on metre sticks to show the early decimals of the sequence. Emphasize that those past 1 are longer than one metre.

▸ Provide each child with a copy of **PCM 4**. Ask them to write 0·1 in the first frog and then to fill in numbers on the first lily-pad trail by counting on in steps of one-tenth, beginning at zero. The second trail can continue in steps of 0·1 from the last number of the first trail and so on.

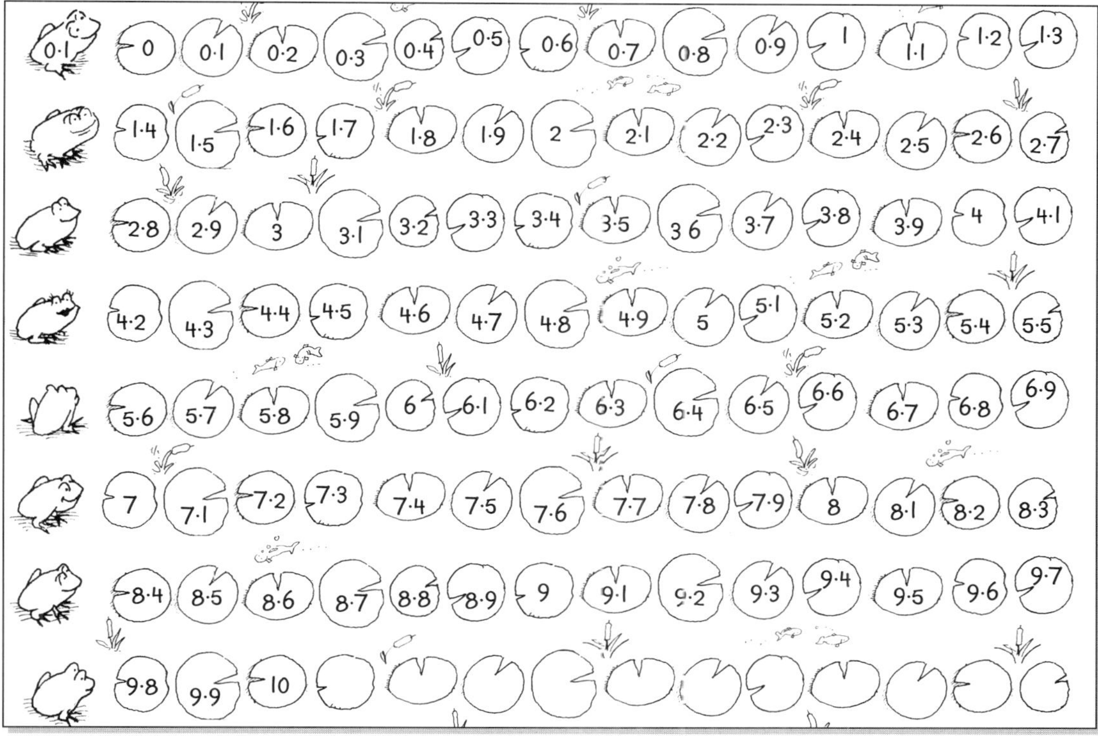

Encourage children to read out the decimals as they write them.

❷ **Order decimals with two places.**
Once the trails have been filled in and children are confident with the pattern of counting in tenths, give pairs of numbers with one decimal place and ask children to say which is larger, for example 0·4 and 3·1. Children can write down the two decimals and circle the larger in each pair. Encourage them to check their answers using their lily-pad number trails.

Feedback

Can each child:
▸ describe and read decimals correctly?
▸ order two-digit decimals, for example 0·4, 0·7, 1·2, 3·8?

Does each child understand the columns to the right of the decimal point, for example tenths and hundredths? Can they tell you what the 3 and the 5 in 3·5 represent?

Does anyone have difficulty counting past whole-number boundaries, for example one-tenth more than 1·9?

Place value, ordering, rounding

Objective

Begin to multiply whole numbers by 100.

Resources

- four large hoops, labelled 'Th', 'H', 'T' and 'U'
- large number cards, with extra 0-cards
- calculators
- 1–100 number cards

What children are learning

to multiply a number by 100 we move the digits
two places to the left and fill the spaces with zeros,
for example:

$$
\begin{array}{ccc}
H & T & U \\
\hline
 & & 4 \quad \times 100\\
4 & 0 & 0
\end{array}
$$

Words you can use

multiply, ten, hundred, digit, place value

Things to note

- Avoid telling children to 'add a zero' when multiplying by 10 or 'add two zeros' when multiplying by 100. These phrases can be confusing for children because we are not actually *adding* anything. We are multiplying. When we do *add* zero to a number the number stays the same, for example $6 + 0 = 6$. Also, this phrase only works for whole numbers and causes confusion when children meet decimals, for example $6{\cdot}2 \times 100 = 620$, not $6{\cdot}200$. Focus attention on the movement of the digits one place to the left when we multiply by 10 and two places to the left when we multiply by 100.
- This lesson begins by revising multiplying by 10.

Activities

❶ **Multiply whole numbers by 10.**
   Set out four large hoops on the floor, labelled 'Th', 'H', 'T' and 'U'. Ask two children to take a large number card each and to stand in the tens and units hoops to make a number, for example 25:

What will happen when we multiply by ten? The digits have to move one column to the left. The two children each jump across into the next hoop. Invite another child to take a 0-card and to stand in the units hoop, making 250. Repeat with several two-digit numbers.

❷ **Multiply whole numbers by 100.**
  ▸ *To multiply by one hundred we need to multiply by ten again.* The children all move across one more hoop to the left. Invite another child to take a 0-card and to stand in the units hoop, making, for example, 2500. Set some more examples, asking children to multiply by 100 in one step. This will entail the two children each moving two hoops to the left and inviting two children to take 0-cards and stand in the tens and units hoops.
  ▸ Give each child a calculator. Ask them to key in a single-digit number, for example 2. *What will happen to this number if we multiply it by a hundred?* Ask the children to write their prediction on paper, for example $2 \times 100 = 200$. Now ask them to key in ⊗①⓪⓪⊜. *Is the answer the same as you thought?* Children should tick or cross their prediction, writing the correct answer if necessary. Discuss any wrong answers. *Why did you think the answer would be that?*
  ▸ When children are confident, ask them to do the same with a two-digit number.
  ▸ Children take turns to take a 1–100 number card. They write their prediction and then multiply the number by 100 on the calculator to check. Draw their attention to the movement of each of the digits two places to the left rather than on the extra zeros in the tens and units columns. *What is happening each time?* This can be seen clearly by entering the chosen numbers and the answers when multiplied by 100 into a table, as shown.

Th	H	T	U
			7
	7	0	0
		1	5
1	5	0	0
		4	2
4	2	0	0

Feedback

Can each child:
  ▸ multiply whole numbers by 10?
  ▸ multiply whole numbers by 100?

Does anyone have difficulty reading four-digit numbers that contain zeros, for example 2700 or 3010?

Can children tell you what each digit is worth?

Objective

Order a set of whole numbers up to 10000.

Resources

- 0–9 number cards
- 20 to 30 cards, each showing a four-digit number

What children are learning

to appreciate the relative sizes of numbers; this is vital if children are to compare and order them

Words you can use

smaller/greater than, less than, more than, order, compare, digit

Things to note

- The idea that the position of a digit in a number determines its worth is known as 'place value'. Place value in our number system allows us to create an infinite series of numbers using just ten digits (0, 1, 2, 3, 4, 5, 6, 7, 8 and 9).
- Children will need to be confident in ordering two- and three-digit numbers before they will be able to tackle four-digit numbers with any assurance. If children struggle with the activities below, do each of them with three-digit numbers before extending to four digits. The activities begin with revision of ordering three-digit numbers.

Activities

❶ **Order a set of whole numbers up to 1000.**
Children choose three 0–9 number cards, for example 5, 2, 9, and arrange them in two different ways, for example 529 and 952. They write down the two numbers and circle the larger number.

$$5 \quad 2 \quad 9 \qquad 9 \quad 5 \quad 2$$

They then rearrange the three number cards again, for example 259 and 592, and for a third time, for example 295 and 925, each time writing down the two numbers and circling the larger number. They then write the six numbers formed in ascending order: 259, 295, 529, 592, 925 and 952.

❷ Order a set of whole numbers up to 10 000.
You will need about twenty number cards, each showing a four-digit number, for example 4608, 6123, 8113, 9568 etc. Each pair will need a large sheet of paper on which you have drawn seven rectangles. Working in pairs, children take four of the number cards, arrange them in order of size and place them on alternate rectangles.

They then have to think of a number to go in each of the empty rectangles which keeps the group of numbers in order of size. Record the order of the group and repeat with new cards.

Feedback

Can each child:
▸ order a set of whole numbers up to 1000?
▸ order a set of whole numbers up to 10 000?
▸ explain how they know one number is larger than another?

Is anyone unsure of how to read/place numbers containing zeros, for example 4020?

Place value, ordering, rounding

Objective
Round any positive integer to the nearest 100.

Resources
- three-digit number cards (or numbers written on slips of paper)
- 0–1000 number line marked in hundreds
- 0–9 number cards

What children are learning
to round any three-digit number to the nearest 100

Words you can use
round, nearest, numbers, hundred, thousand, multiple

Things to note
- By convention, numbers like 150, 250, 350 … are rounded *up* to the nearest hundred, rather than down. Discuss with children that numbers like these are half-way between two hundreds. This can easily be demonstrated on a 0–1000 number line.
- When rounding, children often make the mistake of looking only at the left-hand digit, so they would round 750, 760, 770, 780, and 790 to 700 rather than to 800. To remedy this, the child can position the number on a 0–1000 number line and see the hundreds number that it is nearest to.

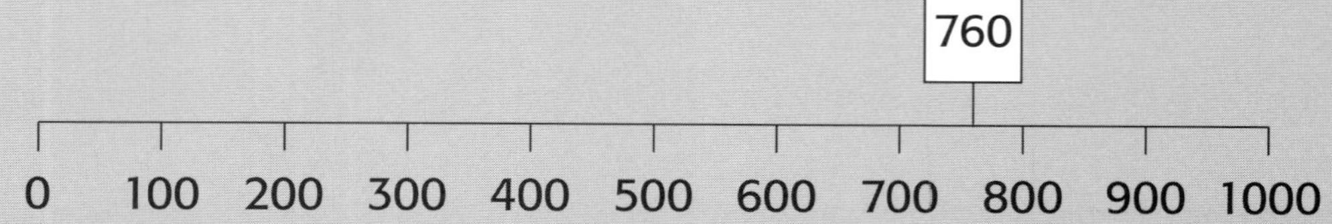

In this way it becomes clear that 760, for example, is closer to 800 than to 700.

Activities
❶ Round three-digit numbers to the nearest 100.
- On a large sheet of paper, draw ten columns labelled 100, 200, 300 … 1000. Ask the children to pick a three-digit number card each. Explain that they must put their number in the column headed by the closest multiple of 100. Encourage them to use a 0–1000 number line marked in hundreds to find the closest multiple of 100. (A metre stick marked 0, 100, 200 … 1000 can be used.)

Remind them that this process is called *rounding*. Children should continue to pick cards and place them appropriately. If children find this difficult, ask them to place each number on the number line first. *Which multiple of a hundred is your number nearest to?*

▸ Ask children to work in pairs. Each pair needs two sets of 0–9 number cards shuffled together. Ask each child to write a list of the multiples of 100 up to 1000. The children take turns to choose three number cards and arrange them to form a three-digit number, for example 742. The number created should be rounded to the nearest hundred and written next to the nearest multiple of 100. That multiple of 100 can then be crossed out on the child's list. The winner is the first child to cross out all the numbers on their list.

100
200
300
400
500
600
7̶0̶0̶ 742
800
900
1000

▸ Ask children to make a list of the multiples of 100 to 1000 as in the above activity. Call out a three-digit number, for example *two hundred and eighty-one*. Children cross the nearest multiple of 100, in this case 300, from their list. Concentrate on numbers that appeared to cause difficulty in the earlier activities, particularly numbers ending in 50.

▸ Give some practical examples, for example *There were 871 people at the match. Roughly how many were there? My holiday cost about £400, rounded to the nearest £100. How much might it have cost exactly?* (between £350 and £449)

Feedback

Can each child:

▸ round three-digit numbers to the nearest 100?
▸ identify which two multiples of 100 lie either side of a three-digit number?

Does anyone have difficulty placing with reasonable accuracy a three-digit number on the 0–1000 number line marked in hundreds?

Objective

Add or subtract the nearest multiple of 10 and adjust.

Resources

- place-value strips and frame made from **PCM 2**
- copy of **PCM 8** for each child

What children are learning

- to add a near multiple of 10 by adding the nearest multiple of 10 and adjusting
- to subtract a near multiple of 10 by subtracting the nearest multiple of 10 and adjusting

Words you can use

plus, add, total, altogether, more, take away, subtract, minus, equals, makes, tens, units, digit

Things to note

- 'Near multiples of 10' are numbers on either side of and close to 10, 20, 30 etc., for example 19, 21, 28, 32 etc.
- To develop the strategy covered in this lesson children need to be able to add and subtract 10 and multiples of 10 confidently. Ensure children appreciate that the units/ones digit in a number remains the same as 10, 20, 30 etc. is added or subtracted, for example $8 \rightarrow 28$ or $54 \rightarrow 14$.
- The strategies that work for adding and subtracting 9, 11, 19, 21, 29, 31 etc. will also work for larger 'near multiples of 10'. The word 'adjusting' is sometimes used to describe the final subtraction or addition of one.
- Use a variety of the vocabulary listed above to ensure that children experience a wide range of words for addition and subtraction.
- Children often have difficulty deciding whether any 'adjusting' should be addition or subtraction. For example, when subtracting 19 from 53 they often subtract 20 and then subtract (rather than add) a further one, giving an answer of 32. Explaining the question in a context can help, for example *I have fifty-three sweets and I want to give nineteen to my friend. I give them twenty but then take back one.*

Activities

❶ Add and subtract multiples of 10.

Using the four 0–9 number strips and the rectangular frame made from **PCM 2**, show the number 3745. *What number does this show? What number would be ten more than this number? What would be twenty more than this number?* Move the tens digits to show that when adding ten or twenty only the tens digit changes. Repeat for adding other multiples of 10, for example 30, 40. *What if our starting number was 3795 and we added ten or twenty?* Demonstrate adding ten or twenty where a hundreds boundary is crossed. Repeat for subtracting multiples of 10 in the same way.

		9	
9		8	
8		7	9
7	9	6	8
6		5	7
Th	**H**	**T**	**U**
3	7	4	5
1	5	2	3
0	4	1	2
	3	0	1
	2		0
	1		
	0		

❷ Add and subtract the nearest multiple of 10 and adjust.

▸ Before copying **PCM 8** write some two-digit numbers in the top left-hand circles of the crowns. Give each child a copy of the PCM. Show how to use the crowns to add near multiples of 10 such as 29, 31, 49, 51 etc. Point out that it is easier to add multiples of 10 first and then to adjust. *Twenty-one is near to twenty, so first we add twenty and then adjust.* Demonstrate that following around the bottom line of the crown will lead you to the same answer as going along the top of the crown. If necessary, use the place-value strips to demonstrate adding 21 by adding 20 and then adding 1. Encourage children to talk through each strategy, for example 'to subtract nineteen, it is easy to subtract twenty but then we have subtracted too many so we have to put one back'. Ask children to fill in the circles of the crowns.

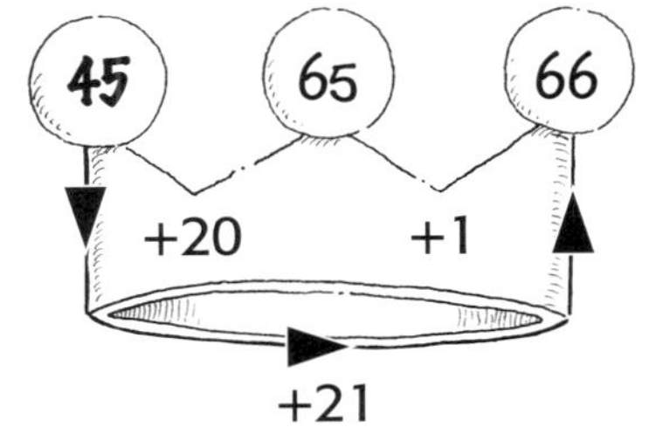

▸ Finish by asking questions about their answers and how they worked them out, for example *What is forty-eight plus thirty-nine? How did you work it out?*

▸ *Variation:* for further extension, three-digit numbers can be written into the left-hand circles of the crowns.

Feedback

Can each child:

▸ add or subtract multiples of 10?

▸ add or subtract the nearest multiple of 10 and adjust?

Does anyone have difficulty mentally adding a multiple of 10 to a two-digit number, for example 38 + 40, 69 + 50?

Which children are confident about how to adjust for addition and subtraction?

Pencil and paper procedures (+ and –)

Objectives

Develop and refine written methods for column addition.
Add more than two whole numbers less than 1000.

Resources

▸ none needed

What children are learning

▸ a written method for adding numbers which are too large to add mentally
▸ to add more than two numbers using a written method
▸ to approximate before calculating

Words you can use

sum, total, number, order, addition, check, add

Things to note

▸ Children will naturally approximate before calculating to give themselves an idea of whether the numbers they are considering are suitable.
▸ Children should be able to add any two-digit numbers mentally before being introduced to standard written methods for addition.
▸ The activities on this sheet allow children to work in whichever way is appropriate for them. This may involve working mentally and jotting things down informally, for example:

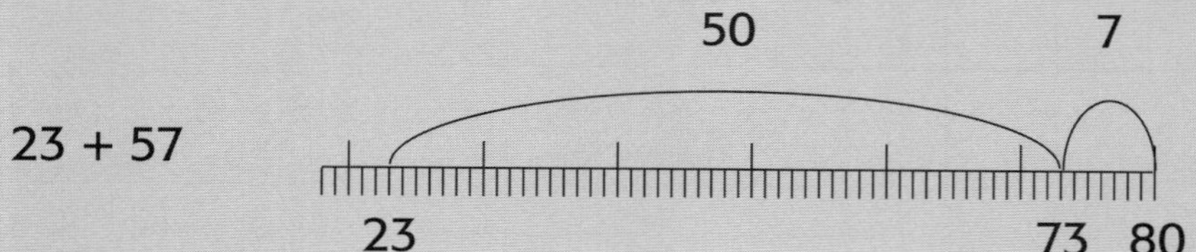

or using a more formal method, for example:

```
   23
 + 57
 ----
   70
   10
 ----
   80
```

Activities

❶ Add more than two whole numbers less than 1000.

▸ Write about twelve single-, two- and three-digit numbers on the board, for example 27, 134, 9, 529, 99, 201, 7, 628, 45, 16, 63, 312. Ask children to work in pairs or in groups of three. They have 3–4 minutes to choose numbers to add together to get as close to a target number as possible. *I'm going to set you a target number. You can add as many of these numbers as you like to get as close to the target as you can. The first target number is 620.* The group compare answers and the child whose answer was

529	312	45
88	201	134
+ 7	+ 134	+ 437
500	600	500
100	40	100
24	7	16
624	647	616

nearest to the target wins a counter. A second counter can be awarded if the target is hit exactly. Children who are equally close get a counter each. Further targets can include 500, 750, 462, 380 etc. The winner of each round could announce the target for the next round.

▸ Children can be set different tasks, including winning a counter for:
  - reaching a total between 370 and 400 or between 370 and 380
  - finding three numbers that give a total of 327 (27 + 99 + 201) or 420 (45 + 63 + 312).

▸ *Variation:* children can work with single- and two-digit numbers only. Write 56, 92, 4, 63, 13, 8, 53, 47 on the board. Ask children to add three numbers to get as close as possible to targets such as 80, 150, 190 etc.; to make a total between 80 and 90 or between 200 and 210; to find which three numbers have a sum of 68 (56 + 4 + 8), 104 (53 + 47 + 4), 172 (56 + 53 + 63), 192 (92 + 47 + 53) etc.

Feedback

Can each child:
▸ add three whole numbers less than 100 using a written method?
▸ add three whole numbers less than 1000 using a written method?

Did children estimate answers to help get as close as possible to the target numbers?

Objective

Recognize multiples of 2, 3, 4, 5 and 10 up to the tenth multiple.

Resources

- empty 4 × 4 grids
- empty 5 × 5 grids
- counters

What children are learning

- to understand and use the word 'multiple'
- to recognize the multiples of 2, 3, 4, 5 and 10 up to the tenth multiple

Words you can use

odd, even, count on, count back, twos, pairs, multiples, difference, digit, multiple

Things to note

- A 'multiple' is a number that another divides into without a remainder, for example multiples of 2 are numbers that, when divided by two, have no remainder. Children may learn multiples as 'answers to the times tables', for example multiples of 2 are the answers to the 2 times table. However, it is important that children realize that numbers beyond the times table can be multiples too, for example multiples of 2 include numbers beyond twenty such as 68 and 432.

Activities

❶ Recognize multiples of 2, 3, 4, 5 and 10 up to the tenth multiple.

- Begin to list multiples of 2, 5 and 10 on the board, reminding children of the word 'multiple', for example multiples of 2: 2, 4, 6, 8, 10, 12 … Ask children to continue to say the multiples of 2, 5 and 10 and discuss the patterns within these sequences, for example *All the numbers are even … They all end in a zero or a five … They all end in zero* etc. Draw attention to numbers that are multiples of 2, 5 and 10, that is the numbers that appear in all three lists.

- Provide each child with a 4 × 4 grid or ask them to draw their own on squared paper. Each child should copy some of the numbers listed on the board into the grid. Call out the number two, five or ten, for example *The number is five*. Each child must choose a number from their grid that is a multiple of the number called out. Each should declare the number chosen as a multiple of this number, for example 'The number twenty on my grid is a multiple of five'. Talk through each child's number and, if correct, the child covers the number with a counter. Continue to call out two, five or ten until a child has covered all the numbers on their grid. Encourage children to notice that some multiples are better to include in the grids because they can be covered with a counter as a multiple of 2, 5 or 10, for example 20.

16	20	14	5
8	6	25	12
100	20	90	10
45	18	30	70

- Introduce multiples of 3 and 4 on the board, discussing those numbers that are multiples of both 3 and 4, for example 12. Encourage children to count on in threes and fours to generate the lists up to 30 and 40, respectively. Ask children to choose and copy some of the multiples of 2, 3, 4, 5 and 10 into a 5 × 5 grid. Repeat the game above, explaining that the winner will be the first child to get five counters in a line, horizontally, vertically or diagonally.
- Give children a number, for example *twenty-four*. Ask them to think of statements they can make about the number and then collate a list on the board: It is even. It is a multiple of four. It is one less than twenty-five. (Restrict 'less/more than' statements to one for each number.) How many statements can the group make?

Feedback

Does each child recognize multiples of 2, 3, 4, 5 and 10 up to the tenth multiple?

Which numbers do children confidently identify as multiples?

Understanding multiplication and division

Objective
Round up or down after division.

Resources
cubes, counters, boxes, coins etc. for sharing activities (see below)

What children are learning
- to find remainders after division
- to realize that in some situations giving an answer with a remainder is not appropriate
- to decide whether to round an answer up or down depending on the context

Words you can use
divide, share, shared between, lots of, groups of, equals, remainder, left over, round

Things to note
- Encourage children to make an estimate of what they think the answer to each division might be, for example *Twelve divided by five is about two*. This will help them to develop a feel for answers when dividing.
- There are two main types of division questions, involving either rounding up or rounding down, illustrated here using the question $55 \div 10 = 5$ r 5. Situations that involve rounding *up* are often of the type 'How many of something will be needed to hold something?', for example *How many minibuses will be needed to transport fifty-five children if each bus holds ten children?* (six) Situations involving rounding *down* are often of the type 'How many of something can I get/make with something?', for example *How many 10p chews can I buy with 55p?* (five)
- Children need opportunities to discuss these problems, focusing carefully on the exact question to determine whether to round the remainder up or down. It is better to talk through a few problems in detail than to rush through lots superficially.

Activities
❶ Divide and give answers with remainders.
Write five division questions on the board, for example $26 \div 5 =$, $32 \div 10 =$ etc. Encourage the children to read each question aloud, for example 'twenty-six shared between five equals?' or 'twenty-six divided by five is … '. If necessary, provide counters or cubes to help children to find and record the questions and answers with remainders, for example $26 \div 5 = 5$ r 1. Suggest that, if working practically, children share twenty-six cubes between five 'people' or into five equal sets. Remind children to use the letter 'r' for the amount left over – the remainder.

Some children may be able to use their knowledge of times tables to work out the answers. Encourage these children to explain their thinking, for example 'I know that five times five is twenty-five so the answer must be five remainder one.'

❷ Round up after division.
Ask questions that use a range of vocabulary and require them to use their recorded division sentences, for example *What is the answer to thirty-seven divided by/shared between four? How many groups of four can be made from thirty-seven and how many are left over?* Now take each question in turn and introduce a context that requires rounding up, for example:
- *If this box holds five sweets, how many boxes would I need to hold twenty-six sweets?*
- *If I can carry five bags at a time, how many trips would I need to make to carry in twenty-six bags from my car?*
- *If a car holds five people, how many cars do I need for twenty-six people?*

Ask children to represent each problem with cubes and boxes or with drawings:

Discuss the answers to the questions. Emphasize, for example, that because there are sweets/people/bags left over, you need another box/car/trip.

❸ Round down after division.
Now take each question in turn and introduce a context that requires rounding down:
- *If I have 26p, how many 5p sweets can I buy?*
- *If there are twenty-six people, how many teams of five can we make?*
- *If I put twenty-six pencils into bundles of five, how many bundles can I make?*

For each of these questions, ask the children to model the situation with cubes and boxes or drawings, as above, and to explain the answer. For example, *You have enough money to buy five sweets, but you don't have enough to buy one more.*

Feedback

Can each child:
- ▸ find remainders after division?
- ▸ realize that in some situations giving an answer with a remainder is not appropriate?
- ▸ decide whether to round an answer up or down depending on the context?

Which methods did children use to calculate division: sharing/grouping/knowledge of times tables?

Which children can identify whether to round up or down, basing their decision on the language of the question?

Objectives

Use relationship between multiplication and division.
Use known facts to multiply and divide.

Resources

▸ 1–10 number cards
▸ sign cards (×, ÷ and =)
▸ blank cards
▸ counters

What children are learning

▸ that multiplication is the opposite, or inverse, of division, and vice versa
▸ that a division statement has a matching multiplication statement that will 'undo' it,
  for example $20 \div 5 = 4$ and $4 \times 5 = 20$
▸ to use their knowledge of multiplication and division facts to answer new questions

Words you can use

multiply, times, lots of, divide, share, makes, equals

Things to note

▸ Children often have difficulty with missing-number questions, particularly those that
  are not necessarily solved using the operation shown, for example $\triangle \div 5 = 4$, which
  might be solved using multiplication rather than division.
▸ Children should realize that multiplication is the opposite, or inverse, of division, and
  vice versa. This means we can 'undo' multiplication with division, and vice versa, so
  $4 \times 3 = 12$ and $12 \div 4 = 3$ etc. If we know one number sentence we can work out
  three more by rearranging the numbers. For example, if we know $4 \times 3 = 12$ we can
  create the multiplication sentence $3 \times 4 = 12$ and the division sentences $12 \div 4 = 3$
  and $12 \div 3 = 4$.
▸ We often solve division questions by using our knowledge of multiplication. For
  example, to solve $24 \div 4$ we ask 'How many fours make twenty-four?'

Activities

❶ **Use the relationship between multiplication and division. Use known facts to
   multiply and divide.**

   ▸ From a set of 1–10 number cards, select two cards and arrange them with a
     × card and an = sign to make a multiplication sentence from the 2, 3, 4, 5 or 10
     times table, placing a blank card to represent the answer.

▸ Ask the children to write the sentence in their exercise books. Rearrange the cards to create a division sentence using the same numbers, for example:

If this was the question we started with, how would we work it out? Discuss that even though this is a division question, we could work it out using multiplication.

▸ Change the two number cards to create new missing-number division questions, for example $\square \div 4 = 8$, $\square \div 10 = 4$ etc. Encourage children to read these aloud as, for example, 'A number when divided by four gives eight'. Ask children to answer and record these questions on paper, describing how they worked each one out, for example 'I multiplied four by eight to get thirty-two'.

▸ Ask each child to write up to ten multiplication and division facts on a sheet of paper. Encourage them to write them large enough so that each number could be covered with a counter. They can choose from facts they already know, or copy the facts from lists. Working in pairs, children take turns to cover with a counter any number; their partner then has to identify the hidden number. *How did you work it out? Did you multiply or divide? Which other fact did you use to work this out?*

$$5 \times \bigcirc = 20$$

Feedback

Does each child appreciate that multiplication and division are inverse operations?

Can each child:
▸ say a matching multiplication statement that will 'undo' a given division statement, for example $20 \div 5 = 4$ and $4 \times 5 = 20$?
▸ use their knowledge of multiplication and division facts to answer new questions?

Is any child uncertain about the order of the numbers when rearranging multiplication statements from division statements, for example writing $5 \times 4 = 20$ and $5 \div 20 = 4$?

53

Pencil and paper procedures (× and ÷)

Objective
Develop and refine written methods for TU ÷ U.

Resources
- 10–50 number cards
- number dice

What children are learning
- to divide a two-digit number by a single-digit number, including answers with remainders
- to show on paper how they worked this out

Words you can use
divide, shared between, multiply, divided by, tables fact, inverse, method

Things to note
- Children should be confident with dividing numbers mentally before beginning to divide numbers using a formal written method, for example setting their work out vertically in columns. For the activities on this sheet children can use mental methods, informal methods or formal written methods. Ask the teacher which methods s/he would like the children in your group to use and adjust the lesson appropriately. Children in the group can tackle the questions in different ways if necessary.
- Encourage children to answer division questions using their knowledge of tables facts where possible, rather than working practically.

Activities
❶ Divide a two-digit number by a single-digit number.
- Write the division sign on the board and ask children what it means. *What words do we say when we see this sign?* Write a division question without a remainder and describe it using the words 'divided by' and 'shared between', for example $45 ÷ 5 = \square$. *Forty-five divided by/shared between five equals?* Encourage children to answer the question using their knowledge of tables facts, or practical materials, if necessary. *How many fives make forty-five?*

Introduce a question that involves a remainder, for example $46 \div 5 =$. Invite children to show and explain how they would work this out and to record this on paper, for example 'I know that five times nine is forty-five so forty-six divided by five is nine remainder one'. ($46 \div 5 = 9$ r 1) Or, 'Forty-six sweets shared between five people means each person gets nine sweets, with one left over'.

▸ Working in pairs, children pick a 10–50 number card as the number to be divided, for example 42. They then roll a dice to get a single-digit number, for example 5. Working separately, the children divide the two-digit number by the single-digit number giving an answer with a remainder, for example $42 \div 5 = 8$ r 2. Children should compare answers and record on paper the question, the answer and how they worked it out. Encourage the children to describe each statement recorded as, for example, 'Forty-two divided by five is eight remainder two'.

Variations: children can work as a whole group to answer each question and compare answers. If children are successful in the above activity, increase the number cards to 10–100.

▸ Discuss how to tackle a division calculation in which the number is higher than the known multiplication facts, for example $42 \div 3$. *We can think of this as 'How many threes are in forty-two?' What are ten threes? Thirty. So this will give an answer bigger than ten. We want to split forty-two into groups of three. Ten groups of three would make thirty. What is left? (12) How many threes in twelve? So forty-two is ten threes plus four threes, which is fourteen threes.* On the board write:

$10 \times 3 = 30$, $42 - 30 = 12$

$4 \times 3 = 12$

$42 = 14 \times 3$, so $42 \div 3 = 14$

Feedback

Can each child:

▸ divide a two-digit by a single-digit number, including answers with remainders?
▸ show how they worked this out on paper?

Are children able to answer straightforward division calculations using multiplication facts?

Who could explain how to work out a division where the answer is more than ten?

54

Fractions and decimals

Objective

Recognize the equivalence of decimal and fraction forms of one-half, one-quarter and tenths.

Resources

- metre stick
- base-10 apparatus
- cards marked '$\frac{1}{10}$', '$\frac{2}{10}$' etc.
- cards marked '0·1', '0·2' etc.
- 10×10 pieces of squared paper

What children are learning

- to appreciate that although fractions and decimals look very different, they stand for the same thing
- to know that 0·5 is equivalent to (the same as) $\frac{1}{2}$, that 0·25 is equivalent to $\frac{1}{4}$, that 0·75 is equivalent to $\frac{3}{4}$ and that 0·1 is the same as $\frac{1}{10}$ etc.

Words you can use

fraction, decimal, equivalent, half, quarter, divide, whole, equal, parts, tenth

Things to note

- Children need to realize that fractions and decimals are different ways of expressing the same amount. For example, $\frac{3}{10}$ and 0·3 are just different ways of writing three-tenths. Rather than treating fractions and decimals as separate topics we need to stress this relationship. Talking about fractions and decimals as different 'languages' can help children to understand this. In the same way that 'Good day!' and 'Bonjour!' are different ways of saying the same thing, the same is true of $\frac{1}{2}$ and 0·5 etc.
- Ensure children do not say 'nought point *twenty five*' to describe 0·25 etc. It is important that children say the digits separately, for example 'nought point *two five*'.
- Language is important in making sense of fractions and decimals. Encourage children to read both aloud, saying, for example, $\frac{2}{5}$ as 'two-fifths'; 0·4 as 'nought point four'.

Activities

❶ **Shade halves, quarters and tenths of shapes.**

Show the children a metre stick. Take a base-10 rod. *What fraction is this?*
If children are unsure, place ten rods along the metre stick. Count up in tenths together as you place the rods: *One tenth, two tenths … one whole. How do we write these?* Place cards showing $\frac{1}{10}$, $\frac{2}{10}$ … along the top of the metre stick.

How do we say one-tenth as a decimal? Write 0·1 on the board as you say *Nought point one. This means no whole numbers and one tenth. The column after the decimal point represents tenths.* Count together in decimals as you point to each tenth along the metre rule: *Nought point one, nought point two ...* Place the cards marked '0·1', '0·2' etc. below the metre rule.

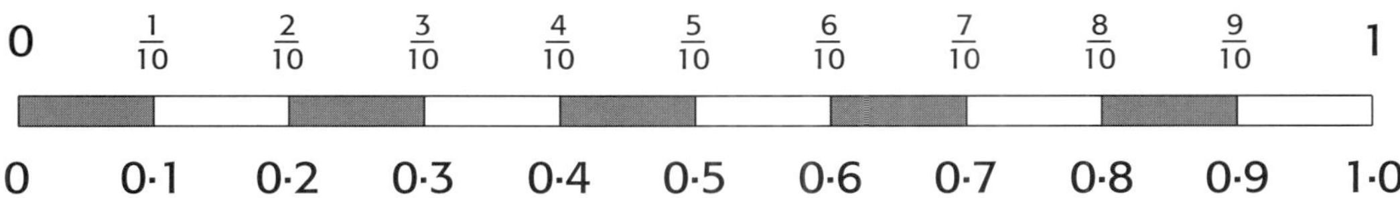

How do we say three-tenths as a decimal? Where is half way along the line? Can you tell me different ways of saying a half? (five-tenths, nought point five)

❷ Recognize the equivalence of decimal and fraction forms of one-half, one-quarter and tenths.

Give children the 10×10 pieces of squared paper and ask them to prepare the cards for the next game by colouring a different fraction on each piece: quarter, half, three-quarters, tenth, two-tenths etc.

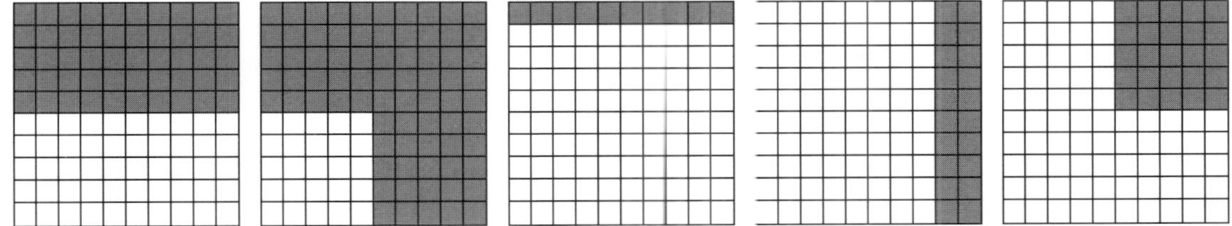

Shuffle the pieces and put them face down in a pile. Children then play the game in pairs. One child should be 'decimal' and the other 'fraction'. As a square is turned over, the 'fraction' child says the fraction shown and records it as a fraction, then the 'decimal' child says and records the fraction as a decimal. For example, the 'fraction' child says 'one-half' and writes $\frac{1}{2}$; the 'decimal' child says 'nought point five' and writes 0·5. If correct, each child can score a point. They swap roles after every four cards so that both children practise describing amounts as fractions and decimals.

Feedback

Does each child:

▸ appreciate that although fractions and decimals look very different, they stand for the same thing?

▸ know that 0·5 is equivalent to (the same as) $\frac{1}{2}$, that 0·25 is equivalent to $\frac{1}{4}$, that 0·75 is equivalent to $\frac{3}{4}$ and that 0·1 is the same as $\frac{1}{10}$ etc?

Which children can confidently rewrite $\frac{3}{10}$ in decimal form?

Which children can confidently rewrite 0·7 in fraction form?

Mental calculation strategies (+ and –)

Objective
Add/subtract mentally any pair of two-digit whole numbers.

Resources
- counters in two colours

What children are learning
to add and subtract any pair of two-digit whole numbers

Words you can use
add, plus, total, sum, difference, subtract, minus, equals

Things to note
- Remind children of some of the strategies for adding and subtracting mentally, for example doubling and halving, using 'near multiples of 10', partitioning etc.
- This activity encourages children to do several mental calculations before committing themselves to a pair of numbers. Encourage children to identify a target number in the grid and then try to find two numbers that give the number, rather than simply choosing pairs of numbers at random. This becomes particularly important as squares are covered during the game.
- Encourage children to use a variety of language, including 'add', 'plus', 'total', 'sum', 'difference', 'subtract', 'minus', 'equals'.
- Encourage children to discuss the most appropriate strategies for adding/subtracting 'near multiples of 10'.
- This game can be played several times during the year to provide practice in adding and subtracting two-digit numbers.

Activities

❶ Add/subtract mentally any pair of two-digit whole numbers.

On the board draw a bag containing the numbers shown. Alongside draw a 4 × 4 grid with the numbers shown below. Children can work in pairs; each pair will need to copy the grid onto paper to use as their gameboard. The first player chooses two numbers from the bag and decides whether to add or find the difference between the numbers. If the answer is on the grid they cover it with a counter in their colour. The first player to get three in a line vertically, horizontally or diagonally wins. Children can use a calculator to check answers. As the game develops, encourage children to choose a number on the grid that it would be useful to cover and to think carefully about which two numbers might hit that number. It might be necessary to impose a time limit on each go, but make sure that you give children enough time to do several mental calculations in order to get their chosen number. Encourage children to make informal jottings to help them.

27	87	12	17
65	70	84	92
7	109	57	114
154	22	43	42

▶ *Variations:* children can work together to find all the numbers in the grid. *Which numbers were easiest to get? Which were hardest? Why? Which numbers are you still trying to get? Do you think you will need to add two numbers to get it or subtract them? Why?* Change the numbers in the bag and in the grid to provide a second game. If children find this game too difficult, use smaller numbers and restrict the game to either addition or subtraction. Alternatively, play the game as a whole group and aim to cover all the numbers.

Feedback

Can each child:

▶ add mentally any pair of two-digit whole numbers?

▶ subtract mentally any pair of two-digit whole numbers?

Do children choose an appropriate strategy for the numbers they have picked, for example for 36 + 29 do they use 'near multiple of 10', adding 30 and taking away 1?

Do children use approximation skills to identify two numbers with a difference/total of a certain target?

add 400	plus 70	increase by 9
add 800	plus 7	increase by 90
add 80	plus 500	increase by 6
add 600	plus 8	increase by 60
minus 600	subtract 50	decrease by 9
minus 70	subtract 500	decrease by 6
minus 60	subtract 8	decrease by 700
minus 400	subtract 80	decrease by 7

9	9	9	9
8	8	8	8
7	7	7	7
6	6	6	6
5	5	5	5
4	4	4	4
3	3	3	3
2	2	2	2
1	1	1	1
0	0	0	0

Th	H	T	U

A postman delivers 16 parcels on Monday and 17 on Tuesday. How many parcels does he deliver?	Peter has 28 sweets. Jo has 19 more. How many sweets has Jo?  
36 people live in my street. 4 people live in each house. How many houses are there? 	Sue has 29 fewer sweets than Megan. Megan has 37 sweets. How many has Sue?
An octopus has 8 legs. How many legs do 4 octopuses have? 	Amy has 26 stickers and Nagajan has half as many. How many stickers do they have in total?
I am on a 48 km journey and have already travelled 17 km. How far have I still to go?	John has 30 football cards. He loses half of them. How many does he have now?
There are 24 children in the class. One third of them are boys. How many are girls? 	100 people are at a party. Half of them are adults. How many are children? 
There are 74 children on a school trip. 59 children have brought sandwiches. How many have not brought sandwiches?	In my road 4 people live in each house. There are 8 houses. How many people live in my road?

260	180	720	980	420
480	680	840	400	160
700	300	100	620	240
460	380	860	40	320
600	1000	740	880	560
960	140	20	640	900
340	220	760	360	540
80	820	500	280	440
800	780	920	120	60
580	940	200	520	660

45p	*The* **Guardian**	£1·25	
£2·99	PENCILS	40p	BESTCO Beans baked in tomato sauce
18p		£2·45	TASTY CUPPA TEA BAGS 48
£4·99		£4·50	Anthology of traditional Folk Tales from Europe
£1·30	FIT BLOKE JULY	37p	MILK Chocky
£2·75	LUXURY PRALINE SELECTION OF BELGIUM	48p	MILK MILK
£2·55	XPERSOFT Loo Rolls	90p	
£3·50	CINEMA SCREEN 1	65p	

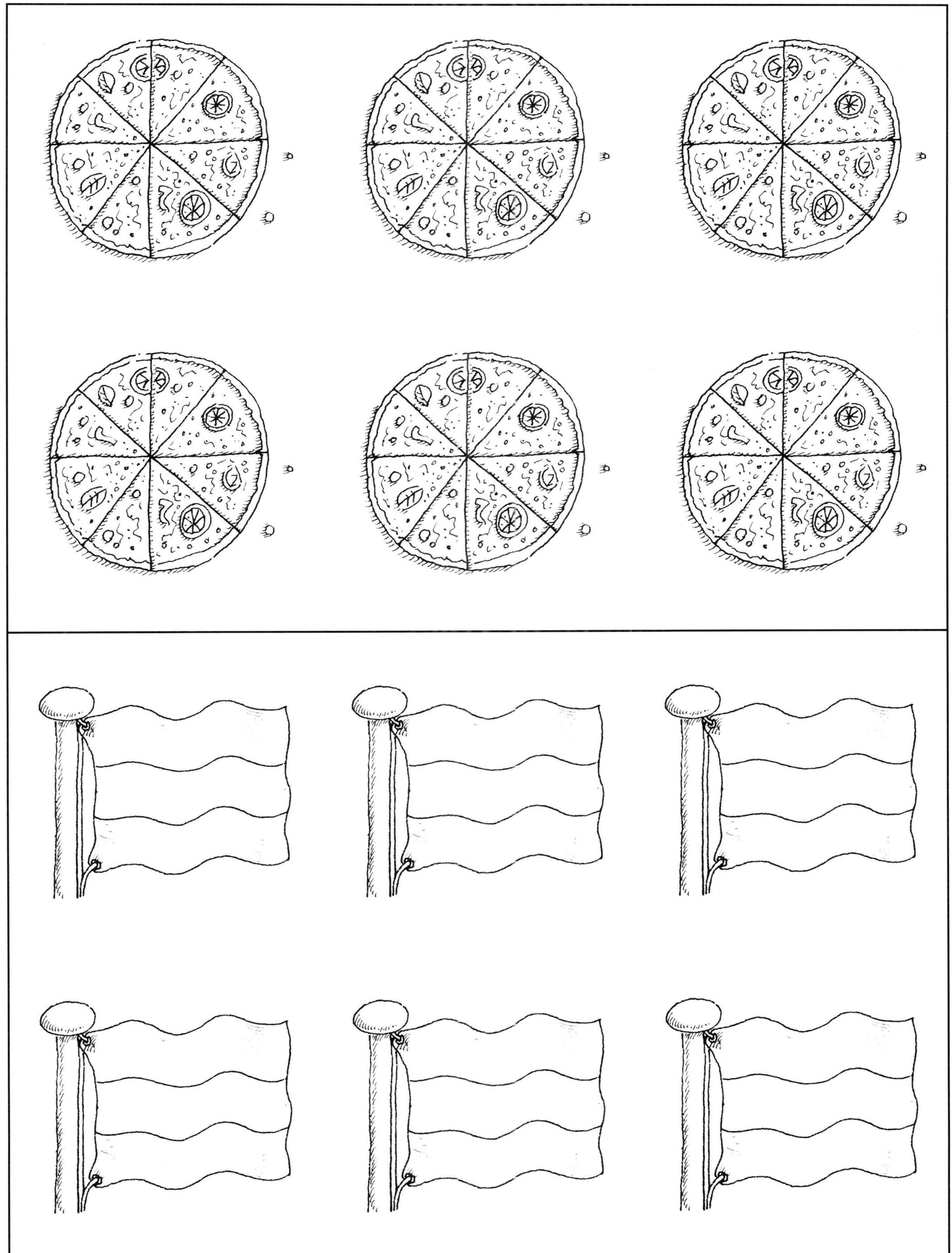

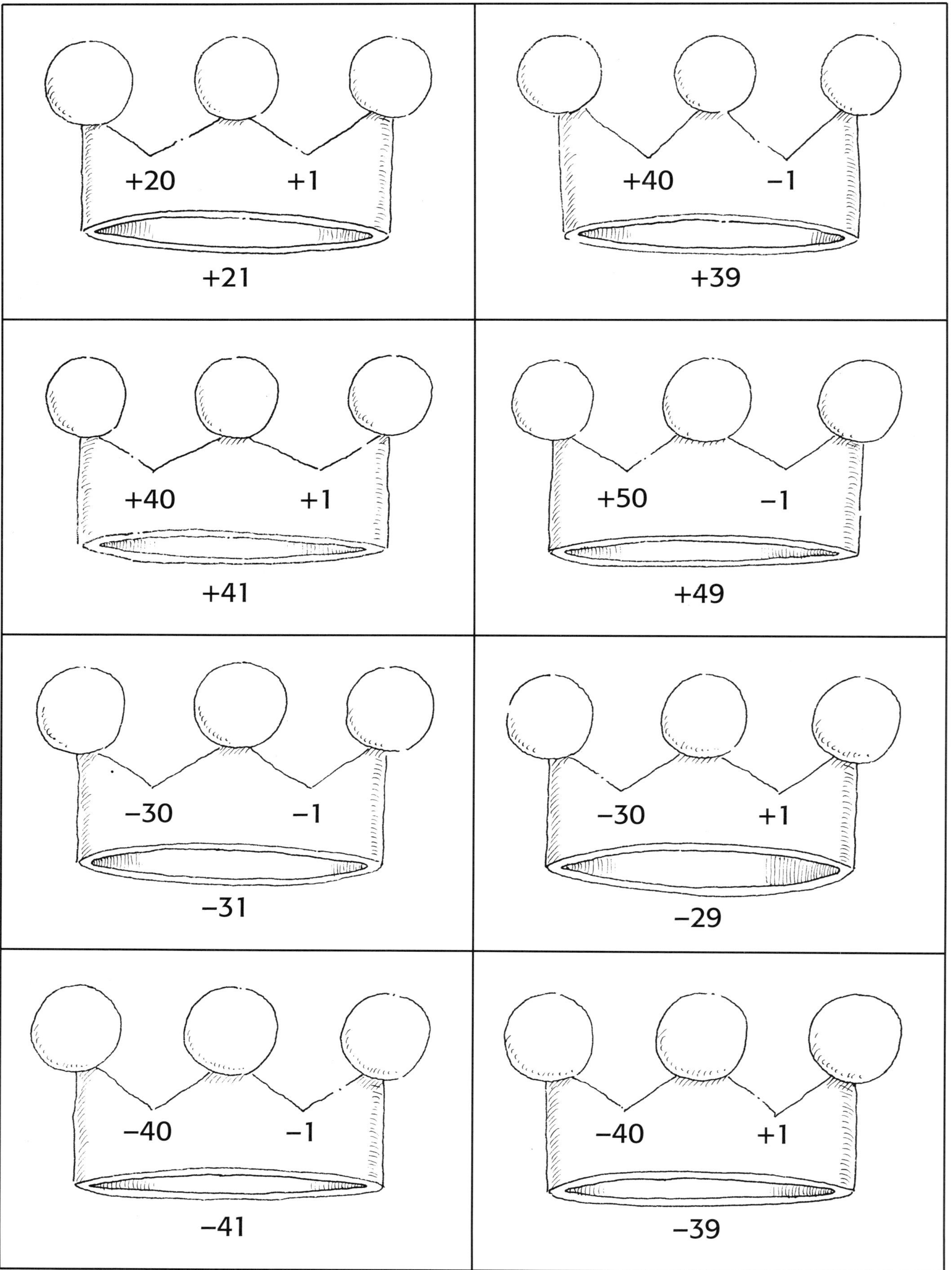

+20   +1
+21

+40   −1
+39

+40   +1
+41

+50   −1
+49

−30   −1
−31

−30   +1
−29

−40   −1
−41

−40   +1
−39